CW01066557

Outcomes

Living Earth Foundation
May 1998

INTRAC NGO Management and Policy Series

Outcomes and Impact:

Evaluating Change in Social Development

Peter Oakley, Brian Pratt and
Andrew Clayton

INTRAC NGO Management and Policy Series No. 6

An INTRAC Publication

INTRAC:
The International Non-governmental Organisation Training and Research Centre
A Summary Description
INTRAC was set up in 1991 to provide specially designed management, training and research services for NGOs involved in relief and development in the South and dedicated to improving organisational effectiveness and programme performance of Northern NGOs and Southern partners where appropriate. Our goal is to serve NGOs in (i) the exploration of the management, policy and human resource issues affecting their own organisational development, and (ii) the evolution of more effective programmes of institutional development and cooperation.

INTRAC offers the complementary services of:
Training;
Consultancy; and
Research

First published in 1998 in the UK by
INTRAC
PO Box 563
Oxford
OX2 6RZ
United Kingdom

Tel: +44 (0)1865 201851
Fax: +44 (0)1865 201852
e-mail: intrac@gn.apc.org

ISBN 1-897748-21-3

Designed and produced by
Davies Burman Associates
Tel: 01865 343131

Printed in Great Britain by
Antony Rowe Ltd., Chippenham, Wiltshire

Disclaimer:
This book has been supported by the Steering Group for the Third International Workshop on Evaluating Social Development. Individual contributions are the responsibility of the contributors and the organisations represented on the Steering Group do not necessarily endorse all the views or opinions expressed in this book.

Contents

Introduction

The current debates that surround the evaluation of development projects are embedded in wider debates about authority, legitimacy, transparency and accountability. (Marsden, Oakley and Pratt 1994)

The above was written in the concluding chapter of *Measuring the Process* published in 1994. Today it seems ever more true that evaluation is closely tied to wider debates about development which is why a single simple 'tools based' approach has failed to take hold despite the effort put into creating a universal solution to our needs for evaluation. Those agencies who feel frustrated by this failure have fallen back on evaluations that do no more than review the efficiency of the delivery of services through specific activities. Evaluation remains controversial. It is controversial within agencies and between agencies. Within agencies the role of the evaluation department and its staff seems constantly to rise and fall, and evaluators still remain very concerned about their position within the structure of their agency. Between agencies the announcement of an evaluation can be almost as bad as calling for battle lines to be drawn up. Need it be so?

We have always argued that the evaluation of social development is an essential aspect of good development but one which requires skill, care and commitment. It requires us to recognise that it is closely related to so many of the issues which continue to be at the core of debates about the nature of development: the nature of power relations between donors and recipients; North/South divides (and now West/East divides as well); about relations between NGOs and other development agencies; and between development agencies and those they pretend or aspire to serve or work with. We cannot think about evaluation without considering these and many other power relations. Evaluation is a reflection of other current debates in society; thus, as we said above, it relates to the nature of legitimacy, accountability and transparency. Who do we speak for? And do we have the right as development workers and agencies to speak for anyone? Within official agencies there are new debates about civil society and governance, whilst NGOs talk about their mandates, their constituencies

1

and legitimacy. Others try to turn development upside down and bring the client or beneficiary to the fore as the driver of development rather than passive recipient. The present book does not try to resolve these and related issues but recognises that evaluation must be flexible in order to accommodate and reflect these wider debates. It also recognises that our approach to evaluation will reflect who we are, who we work for and the specific debates within our cultures and organisations.

WHAT ARE THE ORIGINS OF THE LATEST WORKSHOP?

Since the mid-1980s there has been an unease about the way social development seemed to be giving way to some very narrow views of what constituted development and this was being reflected in some of the thinking about evaluation which was becoming increasingly instrumental and tied to donor needs. In response to this an informed group formed (David Marsden, Peter Oakley, Tony Fernandes, Heinz Knuvener, Brian Pratt) to discuss these issues, and in order to widen the debate we decided to organise an international workshop.

The First International Workshop on the Evaluation of Social Development, was held in Swansea in 1989. At this we brought together about 80 people to examine the concept of social development and its evaluation. During this Workshop, the distinction was made between an evaluation which owes its origins in a scientific or positivistic approach to society and development compared to one following a more relativist or interpretative approach. A great deal of conventional evaluation and development has its origins in this positivistic paradigm, with the underlying belief that science and technology can solve all developmental problems. The success of the Marshall Plan after World War II, the 'green revolution' in the 1960s and the increase in life expectancy and reduction in infant mortality due to various health interventions all seem to prove this thesis. They appear to say that if we can only get our programme right we can, through the application of scientific principles, solve the major issues confronting the world. By contrast, the relativist approach stresses flexibility, pluralism and the tension between different interests. The Workshop also looked at four key areas in evaluation: qualitative indicators; methodology; the role of the evaluator; and partnership.

One of the important conclusions reached during the Workshop was a belief that it is possible to quantify qualitative indicators and that sometimes the distinction between the two was artificial. Other issues arising from this Workshop included: the importance of evaluation as a learning exercise; the importance of allowing for the cultural context in which the evaluation process takes place; questioning the style of an evaluation; the use of external consultants, their

2

qualifications; and problems of using a predetermined programme design. The proceedings were published by Oxfam as *Evaluating Social Development Projects* (Marsden and Oakley 1990).

The second Workshop took place in 1992 at the Centrum Kontakt der Kontinentum near Amersfoot in the Netherlands. This sought to relate some of the ideas developed in the earlier Workshop to a more practical approach. To facilitate this, a smaller workshop was organised with about 35 participants. Drawing upon their own actual experiences, the participants produced guidelines for evaluating social development by using a framework based on four key stages of an evaluation cycle: preparation, execution, analysis and reflection. Key papers and proceedings were published by INTRAC as *Measuring the Process: Guidelines for Evaluating Social Development* (Marsden, Oakley and Pratt 1994). Some of the major issues that arose during the Workshop included:

- the real problem of time and cost, especially for NGOs; the concern that process approaches could be open-ended, time consuming and needed to be carefully examined in order to justify the resources required;
- the continued imbalance between quantitative and qualitative approaches, in part because many evaluators were less familiar with qualitative methods and indicators;
- the reluctance of donors to let the process run without pulling it back into procedural frameworks/strait-jackets and their unwillingness to suspend rigidly predetermined parameters and schedules;
- and the gap between theoretical commitment and operational practice, and the delay in the newly emerging evaluation paradigm actually taking grip.

Both of the above Workshops, and particularly the one in 1992 were heavily attended by Northern and Southern NGOs. One of the conclusions of the 1989 Workshop was that it was largely the NGOs as opposed to the bigger official international development agencies, who were experimenting with alternative approaches to the evaluation of social development. And yet in the 1980s and early 1990s several studies had suggested that NGOs were not universally committed to project evaluation and that indeed they showed several major technical deficiencies (Tendler 1982; Riddell 1990; Smillie 1995; Surr 1995). There would appear therefore, to be a fairly strong case for arguing that, as a whole, and despite some notable exceptions, NGOs have not been as successful as they might have wished in terms of promoting and implementing innovative approaches to project evaluation.

In conclusion it seemed to us that several major areas warranted further review. These included:

- Stakeholder Analysis;
- Impact Evaluation;
- Indicators;
- Culture and Evaluation;
- Capacity-building and Evaluation;
- Organisational Assessment.

THE THIRD INTERNATIONAL WORKSHOP ON EVALUATING SOCIAL DEVELOPMENT

The present book is the result of the Third International Workshop on the Evaluation of Social Development which was held in the Netherlands in November 1996. Our goal was to capture recent thinking and practice regarding social development by inviting a cross-section of people from 24 countries and representing 54 different agencies. The main focus of this Workshop was the evaluation of the **outcomes** and **impact** of social development. We also aimed to ensure that we were providing a forum for debate and the sharing of ideas in general about the evaluation of social development.

The planning for this Workshop began in June 1995 when we held a one-day workshop to review what had happened since the publication of *Measuring the Process* and to identify key areas of concern to NGOs and others engaged in this field. This led us to establish a steering group consisting of representatives from INTRAC, ACTIONAID, Oxfam, Save the Children Fund, Novib, Bilance and PLAN International. This group then invited other agencies and some individuals to the International Workshop to share their experiences of evaluating the impact and outcomes of social development programmes. Furthermore Peter Oakley was commissioned by the group to visit several of the larger international NGOs and to review the literature and project files of these agencies in order to prepare an overview paper of the current practice and philosophy of the evaluation of social development in those agencies. This paper was discussed in the Workshop and a revised version is reproduced as Chapter 2. For this Peter reviewed over 150 evaluations and related documents. A further 40 or so documents, as listed in Appendix 1, were either presented at or produced by the Workshop itself and the current book is based heavily on these.

The three broad objectives of the Workshop were:

1. to provide a forum in which development agencies and individuals involved or interested in the evaluation of social development can make contact and exchange ideas and information on the issues;

4

2. to update current thinking and practice and to assess where we stand at this moment in terms of the relevance of current practice to the demands of the evaluation of social development;
3. to continue the process of the previous two workshops and to focus on the outcome–impact aspects of the evaluation of social development.

We use the terms 'outcomes' and 'impact' to imply respectively the more immediate and the longer-term effects of a social development programme or project. The terms are defined in more detail in Chapter 2 and discussed in operational terms in Chapter 3. We have tried to be consistent in the use of the terms throughout the book, although recognising that some development agencies may apply or use different terms (e.g. effect) in their own practice.

STRUCTURE OF THE BOOK

In preparing this book we followed the method used in the two former books by not reproducing all of the papers as a literal proceedings. Indeed we did not ask people to make formal presentations in the style of an academic conference; rather we asked practitioners to share with us their experience as we did not want to intimidate people unused to preparing formal papers. Thus we have sought to distil from these papers some of the key findings and issues. The book starts with a review of current and past thinking about the nature of social development (Chapter 1) based on the wider literature and some keynote presentations at the Workshop. In this chapter we trace the history of social development and its rescue from being categorised as merely the delivery of certain types of services to be reinstated as at the heart of development as change and transformation. This is followed by Chapter 2 which is the overview paper on 'Evaluating Social Development' produced for the Workshop and amended in the light of discussion and comments received in the Netherlands. Chapter 2 is a non-critical review of much of existing practice and looks at the issues and approaches that have been taken up by a wide range of development agencies. It is then Chapter 3 which takes us through some of the key elements which have emerged as being important and these are grouped around sections on effect and impact, monitoring and indicators. This chapter also reviews some of the impasses and challenges confronting agencies, the overall aim of the chapter being to identify some of the key elements in the ever-strengthening approach to evaluating social development. However, it is still not a set of prescriptions for the future but a summation of best practice.

In Chapter 4 we have summarised some of the case material presented during the Workshop, using a series of case studies which were thought to illustrate best the rich spread of experiences we reviewed. In particular, case studies from organisations which have tried to use innovative methods and approaches. There were many other fascinating cases presented during the Workshop many of which are referred to in other chapters. The full list of case studies and other papers presented at the Workshop can be seen in Appendix 1. Some papers were never formally written up but verbal presentations were recorded by rapporteurs. Finally Chapter 5 attempts to synthesise some of the key findings and lessons from the practice.

THANKS AND ACKNOWLEDGEMENTS

The authors wish to thank all of participants of the Workshop (full list in Appendix 2). Without their enthusiasm, and the time and energy they brought to the Netherlands, this latest contribution to the debates and lessons from the practice of evaluating social development would not have been possible. We also wish to thank our co-conspirators on the steering group: Hugh Goyder (ACTIONAID), Floris Blankenberg (Novib), Ronald Lucardie (Bilance), Margaret Newens (Oxfam UK/I), Caroline Harper (Save the Children Fund UK), Aiden Timlin (SCF UK) and Henk Frankel (PLAN International) for their work in advising and facilitating the Workshop. Their activities were also dependant on the hard work of Paul Ryder who acted as administrator of the Workshop before and during the event. The Workshop itself was enriched by many speakers and presenters, and special thanks to Dharam Ghai (UNRISD) and Max van de Berg (Novib) who gave plenary presentations to set the back-cloth for our discussions, and to the many others who facilitated working groups, acted as rapporteurs, made presentations and participated in the event.
We would also like to thank all those organisations that funded the Workshop, including the travel costs for participants and this publication. The Workshop was made possible through financial support from: Danchurchaid, the Department for International Development (DFID), the Dutch Foreign Ministry, Novib, Oxfam UK/I, PLAN International, and Save the Children Fund UK. This publication was supported financially by Bilance and DFID. Finally thanks to Marie G. Diaz for copy-editing the text.

Peter Oakley
Brian Pratt
Andrew Clayton
Oxford, December 1997

Chapter 1

Revisiting Social Development

INTRODUCTION

For several decades 'development' was understood to be essentially an economic activity; the modernisation theorists of the 1950s and 1960s believed it to be synonymous with per capita growth, industrialisation and economic indicators. But in 1962 the UN Economic and Social Council argued that 'development is growth plus change'; change in turn is social and cultural and it is both 'quantitative and qualitative' (Esteva1992). In the 1960s social development was used broadly and seen to be synonymous with 'human-welfare' and 'well-being' and as such played a supporting role to development as economic growth and technological advance. In the succeeding years advances have been made and 'social development' has achieved a position of some pre-eminence in the apparently continuous search for what Wolfe (1996) calls 'elusive development'. The culmination has been the 1995 UN World Summit on Social Development which was a belated recognition that the world development agenda was no longer rooted exclusively in the notion of economic growth. Other more qualitative goals were equally important in promoting a better, more secure and just livelihood for the many millions still living in poverty.

'Social development' has become a fashionable term in the 1990s with its central premise that development cannot be seen as a limited, sectoral activity but must encompass a wider range of actions to tackle the many complex issues which affect people's ability to play a part in and to benefit from development processes. Much earlier Korten and Alfonso (1981) argued that 'all development is social development' in the sense that people are the central purpose of development, their skills and capacities its critical resource. Throughout the 1980s and early 1990s there has been an increasing recognition that development is more than the physical improvement of a particular context; a 'way of thinking' about development has prevailed wherein people rather than economics and technology are the central focus. Although the evidence suggests that economics and technology still hold sway to a considerable extent, social devel-

7

opment discourse has noticeably pervaded international and national development institutions and the development agenda has been opened up. Carmen (1996) sees this as social development becoming 'demarginalised' and no longer being seen merely as the 'social means towards economic goals'.

While theories of social change can be found in the writings of such influential thinkers as Smith, Hegel, and Marx, for example, substantially the term 'social development' can be traced back to the immediate post-war period and the structuring of the United Nations and other international bodies charged with the development of the 'underdeveloped' areas of the world (Midgley 1995). At that time the emphasis was on the notion of 'social intervention' with its apparatus of the welfare state and planning in what were referred to as the 'industrial countries'. In the then existing colonies, missionary organisations and other charitable bodies had long provided what could be termed 'social services' in the face of colonial governments more committed to extraction and as a response to the growing problems of destitution, homelessness and urban slums. In colonial Africa social development became a mixture of remedial social services and community development, which were the twin arms of colonial administrations seeking to discharge some of the responsibility for the peoples under their control. The strengthening of the United Nations structure in the 1950s and 1960s saw the emergence of social development on international development agendas, albeit in an essentially welfarist mode and couched in such general terms as 'higher standards of living', 'full employment' and 'social progress' and stressing remedial action. UN Economic and Social Commissions were established in different parts of the world and began to promote a broader notion of development. Similarly in the 1970s and 1980s more specialised agencies such as the ILO (Ghai 1977) and the World Bank (1975) came to recognise the 'other face of development' and both to explore and promote the notion of social development, particularly in relation to issues of poverty and people's needs. Meanwhile, and initially with little recognition, the non-government organisations (NGOs) were approaching the term from a radically different perspective, influenced as they were by their conviction of radically different explanations of the problem. By the 1980s and 1990s the term became common currency although open to broad and very different interpretations.

Within that context, this chapter examines the concept of 'social development' as employed in the past ten to fifteen years and identifies its key dimensions. Clearly it will be impossible to arrive at any universally agreed understanding of the term; the intention is to examine social development within what could be called its two major areas of practice – social welfare and empowerment – to show its richness as a development process and the different ways in which this practice is explained.

THE SOCIAL POLICY AND WELFARE TRADITION

The above historical legacy of colonial administration and the emergence of the UN structure were rooted in several decades of seeing poverty and social problems in terms of the formulation of relevant social policy and the provision of social welfare to the neediest. Central to this approach is the notion of the state as responsible for its citizens and the mounting of a social administration to discharge this responsibility. Social policy and social welfare became the twin responses and approaches to 'social problems' in developing countries. Increasing poverty, widespread unemployment, population pyramids with an enormous base of under five-year-olds, changing family patterns, the tensions and disorganisation of burgeoning cities, the limited availability of basic services, internal violence and the increasing vulnerability of children were some of the symptoms of the kinds of chronic social problems which many newly liberated countries confronted. In this context the emphasis was placed on assisting governments to formulate and to implement relevant policies to tackle these issues and whole bureaucracies and (social) administrative structures were created for this purpose (Gardner and Judd 1963). A critical issue in this respect has been the determination of social policy relevant to the contexts and problems of developing countries and not simply modelled on Western, industrialised nations. Given the cultural, political and social heterogeneity, there can be no notion of a global social policy. Furthermore, as developing countries sought to formulate relevant policies, they were inevitably confronted with two major dilemmas (Jones1990).

Firstly, achieving a relationship and balance between **growth** and **welfare**: while clearly growth does raise the incomes of some families, its impact can lead to an increase in inequalities and 'social problems' with which a government will have to contend. The answer to this dilemma in the 1970s was seen as 'Growth with Distribution' both by linking the poor with growth in the economy and by directly supporting productive activities of the poor. Development, it was argued, would 'trickle down' inexorably to the poor; it rarely did! The counter-arguments saw redistribution as reducing the surplus available for investment and also as weakening incentives to the more productive sectors of the economy.

Secondly, the relative priority of investment in human **capital**: the debate as to whether well-resourced social policies and social welfare programmes actually facilitate economic growth by ensuring a more vigorous, healthy and better educated population which would be well placed to provide the labour for economic growth. Indeed the issue of investment in human capital was central to the economies of newly independent nations in the 1960s and became a major plank of support given by a whole range of international donors.

9

The 1970s and 1980s saw an explosion in the literature concerning social development as social policy and social welfare in developing countries (Kuitenbrouwer 1977; Hardiman and Midgley 1982; Macpherson 1982; MacPherson and Midgley 1987). Social welfare was based on a sectoral approach to social problems and the expected role of government in fulfilling its obligations to provide and to manage social services. This situation inevitably gave rise to debate concerning government's role. The 'residualists' argued that government's role should be minimal and the 'substantivists' argued for a greater role as the best guarantee of equity and against exploitation in the free market (Marsden 1990). The literature covers both the broad spectrum of social services – education, housing, health, social security and clean water supply – and the 'client' or recipient; for example, children, the poor, youth, women or the family as a whole. Jones's (1990) study of 'Social Welfare in the Third World' is the most recent comprehensive review of social welfare by sectors, but with a number of refreshing asides on its relationship to broader development processes. In particular he refers to the school of thought which sees social welfare policies in situations of exploitative economic systems and entrenched elite power as 'palliatives', a concession extracted from these elites and as creating a 'false consciousness' in which the true nature of the services as a prop of the capitalist system is concealed behind a veneer of social justice.

Unlike earlier texts of the colonial period which had tended to be essentially prescriptive in the detail of how a particular service should be set up, these latter studies also began to explore the relationship between social policy and social development. Macpherson (1982) noted a significant shift in social policy in the developing world, from one which was peripheral, residual and primarily concerned with responding to the negative consequences of externally determined socio-economic change, to one which equated social policy with social development. The significant shift was the result of social policy's increasing focus on the 'distributive principle' and a concern with the causes of poverty, inequality and access to resources for development. Social policy is concerned with the distribution of social resources; social development is concerned with distribution based on needs.

Macpherson and Midgley (1987) similarly pointed to the shift in emphasis and referred to the 'restructuring' of social policy in developing countries in a way which made it more pro-active and targeted at providing poor people with the means to take the initiative to determine their own development needs. Furthermore the UN referred to 'development social welfare' in a statement as follows:

The central objective of social welfare policy remains the enhancement of human well-being by raising the level of living, ensuring social justice and widening opportunities for people to develop their highest capacities as healthy, educated, participating and contributing citizens. (UN 1989)

More substantially Midgley (1995) has argued that social development is the 'developmental perspective of social welfare'. In this major study Midgley shakes off the clothes of social welfare as short-term remedial actions designed to mitigate the indiscriminate excesses of economic development and sees social development as '. . . a process of planned social change to promote the well-being of the population as a whole in conjunction with the dynamic process of economic development' (p. 25). Social development is inextricably linked with economic development, is interdisciplinary in its focus, essentially progressive in nature and is interventionist. Its fundamental goal is the promotion of social welfare. In this context, social welfare is not seen as merely the provision of social services, but more broadly as the promotion of 'well-being' which, he argues, occurs when social problems are satisfactorily managed, social needs are met and social opportunities are created. Midgley's position in 1995 is a logical progression from his earlier works and seeks to catch the current and more radical winds which he knows are blowing; yet it remains essentially management-orientated and statist. His only mechanism is one of intervention and his proposals are seemingly unaware of the community initiatives and the social movements which are abroad and which are approaching social development not from the building blocks of colonial administration but from the standpoint of negotiation and action. Currently at the community and individual level social policy is still largely concerned with 'welfare through distribution', human resource development and 'safety nets'. At the societal level, however, it is becoming identified with notions of 'social integration', given the existence of an array of diverse forces which are leading to a breakdown of cohesion and trust in many societies

THE TRANSITION

Although it is impossible to draw clear and authoritative lines between the interpretation and practice of social development, it is possible to examine the evolution of the term over a period of time and to note new lines of thinking. As noted above, the social welfare understanding of social development has historical roots in nineteenth-century ideas on social change and the responsibility of the state to undertake remedial action. We have seen the argument of Midgley (1995) that the provision of a range of social welfare services can be seen as 'developmental' in that it provides the basis on which people can begin to take advantage of the opportunities available for their development. While in the 1950s and 1960s the terms 'social welfare' and 'social development' were used almost interchangeably, by the 1970s there was an increasing concern to distinguish between the 'economic' and the 'social' aspects of development strategies and processes (Conyers 1982). The literature of the 1970s referred to the 'social aspects' or the 'social dimensions' of development, even if these aspects were largely couched in terms of the provision of basic services. Initially these 'social' aspects were seen as the 'non-economic' aspects of development programmes and represented the first recognition that development was to do with people and not just technology and infrastructure (Singer and Jolly 1995). These social aspects were expressed in terms such as 'basic needs', 'quality of life' and 'levels of living' and launched the first attempts to measure social development (Baster 1972). Arguments also began to emerge that 'development' was to do with both economic and social 'change' and that this change implied something more than the provision of some minimum infrastructure of basic services. By the end of the 1970s there was an increasingly widespread recognition that development could not be seen in purely economic terms, but equally widespread was a divergence on the meaning of social development.

In the 1970s undoubtedly the major influence which helped to structure and to guide a new genre of social development programmes and projects was the **dependency** school of development thinking. Dependency explanations of underdevelopment employed a different framework of analysis and questions and led to the identification of different sets of problems which would need to be tackled if 'development' was to occur (Frank 1967). The major impediments to development were seen as structural and the result of unequal and exploitative institutionalised relationships at different levels. Underdevelopment was characterised by 'inequalities and imbalances', the subjugation of the 'traditional' by the 'modern' and the domination of nations, regions and peoples by other more powerful counterparts (Foster-Carter 1974; Long 1976). Within the context of this macro-level analysis, the work of Freire (1972, 1974) operationalised an understanding of social development which still lies at the core of much of contemporary practice. Freire's work described and structured a form of social development intervention which has revolutionised the practice. Essentially Freire explained people's underdevelopment as the result of their domination, oppression and exploitation by centuries of different masters which had resulted in a 'culture of silence' in which the oppressed had no voice, no influence and no involvement in the 'development' taking place around them. Freire argued that this culture of silence would need to be broken first if the oppressed were to play a meaningful role in development. Freire's writings have given us the notion of the oppressed as the 'subjects' of their own development,

12

of people's knowledge and skills as valid contributions to development initiatives and of action as fundamental to social development. His writings have had a powerful influence at every level of social development practice.

Writings on social development in the 1980s began to show the influence of the above emerging analyses. Oakley and Winder (1981) examined the concept and practice of social development in the context of a number of Oxfam UK/I supported projects in Latin America and India and showed how processes of conscientisation, organisation and action lay at the heart of project level initiatives designed to create the conditions for poor people to have greater access to and a say in development policies and resources. Korten and Alfonso (1981) and Jones (1981) stressed the central notion of 'putting people first' as the cornerstone, both psychologically and practically, of social development intervention, an affirmation which was echoed in their own distinctive ways by Chambers (1983) and Cernea (1985). Furthermore, Rahman's (1989) call for People's Self Development and the recognition of people's creative abilities to be subjects of their own development; Bhasin's (1985) detailing of the processes of empowering poor women; and Tilakaratna's (1989) exploration of the role and nature of the animator working to promote social development, were all instrumental in helping to translate this emerging vision of social development into operational methodology. Collectively such writings reinforced the view that social development is not a process whereby poor people merely consume the tangible benefits which have been created and delivered by others. Rather it is more a process whereby previously excluded people seek to break out of this exclusion in order to gain access to and begin to play a part in development. Similarly the changing role of development agencies became apparent, as they sought to shake off a 'paternalistic' approach and to adopt a more 'co-operative' or 'supportive' approach to working with local communities. Examining the evolution of the term and the nature of social development in the context of NGO-supported projects, Brown (1994) suggested that there were three 'conceptual foci' around which interpretations could be grouped:

- traditional social welfare and the promotion of social welfare activities in both quantitative and qualitative terms;

- social development as implying a wide range of measures designed to redress the imbalance in the allocation of resources in favour of the poor and the dispossessed; and

- social development in terms of awakening new (or hitherto inexperienced) forms of consciousness.

13

Brown's three interpretations are an admirable summary of the term in the early 1990s. Although the notion of social development as social welfare is confined more to institutionalised service providers, the other two concepts have been consistently translated into operational practice, in different ways and in different contexts by both international and national NGOs. The evolution of social development as signifying some kind of positive action to redress 'imbalances and inequalities' would appear now to be firmly rooted in development discourse. The following box is drawn from a number of statements and documents on social development from a range of development agencies.

Box 1.1 Common Objectives of Social Development Programmes

1. **Poverty reduction:** not just in terms of increased production but also in terms of helping poor people gain access to the resources necessary to sustain their livelihoods.
2. **Human development:** in the sense of better education, health and family planning.
3. **Participation:** the means by which poor people can be directly involved in development processes which could affect their lives, both negatively and positively.
4. **Empowerment:** in the sense of helping poor people to extend their areas of knowledge and perhaps to acquire new skills and abilities which could enable them to better defend and promote their livelihoods.
5. **Women's social and economic development:** and the promotion of gender equity to ensure equal access to resources and development benefits.
6. **People's rights:** as enshrined in written constitutions and democratic processes, and the rights of particularly vulnerable groups such as children, ethnic minorities and refugees.

A further major influence on emerging interpretations of social development in the 1980s and 1990s has been the increasingly influential concept of people's **participation** in development. Indeed the debate and the arguments surrounding the promotion of participation have in many ways mirrored those of social development. In development intervention terms, the 1990s are very much the decade of 'participation', with apparently endless commitments at national, multilateral and NGO levels to promote and to sustain a 'participatory' approach to development. Participation in both a national democratic and structural sense and also in terms of direct involvement in development programmes and projects has become a key framework within which development is designed and promoted and has spawned a vast literature (for example, Burkey 1993; OECD 1994; Stiefel and Wolfe 1994; World Bank 1996). But the term has also been subject to apparently contradictory interpretations. 'Participation in development' continues to refer primarily to the more structuralist analysis of underdevelopment and sees the breaking of poor people's exclusion as fundamental to their achieving a better livelihood; while 'participatory development' has come to suggest a methodology and a technique of development which seeks to involve local people as opposed to being top-down. The divergence essentially is whether participation is seen as an 'end' or as a 'means' of development processes. The debate continues, the differences are fundamental but a common outcome has been to argue that development has to do with people, their right to be involved in development decisions and actions which might affect their livelihoods.

Social development involves more than changing development investment decisions. It is a way of thinking about development in which people rather than technology or economics are the central focus. It calls for new methods of development planning and action, new institutional structures, a balance between analytic and synthetic thought, leadership and a continuous learning process at both individual and institutional levels. Our understanding of the needs and appropriate approaches to addressing them remains imperfect, but a sufficient start has been made to demonstrate that development in which both the purpose and the most critical resource can be more than simply an abstract ideal. (Korten and Alfonso 1981)

TRANSFORMATION AND EMPOWERMENT

The past decade or so has seen the ever-increasing identification of social development with notions of 'transformation' and 'empowerment'. Such an interpretation presupposes an awareness of the dynamics of a particular context and the identification both of different socio-economic groups and also of the relationships between them. In the early 1980s Galjart (1981) fashioned the concept of **counter-development** which he saw as consisting of several processes; the mobilisation of disadvantaged people, their organisation, their participation in decision-making at different levels and their choice of feasible economic activities. This 'alternative development strategy', as he called it, has served to provide a framework for understanding the evolution of thinking on social development. Social development not only involves strategies of delivering and targeting assistance at the poor but is also about promoting positive changes in

15

people's circumstances (Harper, Workshop Paper 4). Social development has become an umbrella term encompassing a series of objectives: the improvement in people's livelihoods, increasing access to resources, the expansion of people's areas of knowledge and experiences and their participation as a right in development processes. Social development is the antidote to a social authoritarianism which allows the poor to suffer and which deliberately infringes on their opportunities for advancement. Development should not be concerned only with economic rationalism but with people's own views on development processes, which will be shaped by their culture, their society and the historical moment (Ghai, Workshop Paper 1). Kaplan (1996) argues that social development is both 'growth and revolution':

[This view] recognises that development is discontinuous and that it does not move continuously on an upward path, but rather moves step wise from one level to the next. Development is a process in time and natural rhythms need to be respected. For development is not growth. While growth may precipitate development, it implies quantitative increase, while development implies a qualitative change in structure. (p. 40)

Rahman (1993), on the other hand, adopts a more purist stance. Essentially he takes a 'creativist' view of social development which he refers to as 'people's self-development'. He sees this as the 'organic evolution of people's collective search for life' and which is not necessarily dependent upon previous macro-structural change:

People's self-development implies changing the relations of knowledge, to restore popular knowledge to a status of equality with professional knowledge and advancing 'organic knowledge' as part of the very evolution of life and not distanced from it. This offers a new role for intellectuals, in initiating 'animation' work with the people to promote their collective self-enquiry and action. (pp. 178–9)

Human dignity, popular democracy, indigenous knowledge and cultural diversity lie at the heart of Rahman's view of social development which is concerned not only with improving the livelihoods of people at the grass-roots level but also that the society as a whole develops in a way which encourages and strengthens social creativity, solidarity and the capabilities to manage social change. Rahman's views were fashioned in his native Bangladesh and have been extremely influential in developing a methodology of intervention consistent with the above ideals. Dey and Westendorff's (1996) summary of social development as promoted by urban community level volunteers in 16 cities

16

throughout the world similarly reflects the above broad ingredients. They found that the two common features of social development in those particular contexts were: (a) local group action, where people come together in a limited geographic space for a specific purpose, and (b) shared identity, which encourages group solidarity and mutual assistance. Furthermore, Van Beuningen and Does (Workshop Paper 11) argue that social development is concerned with three main problem areas:

- the poverty of poor people and their lack of access to the material resources necessary for a decent living;
- the social exclusion of poor people, their lack of access to societal institutions, to networks and to transactional space within the broader society; and
- the fragility of poor people's lives and their lack of capacity to create and to maintain a network of relations, institutions and public spaces.

Social development, therefore, should be concerned with the development among poor and excluded people of **social capital**; that is, to develop the will and the capacity of poor people and poor communities to live together, to function as a society and to create and maintain shared institutions, goods and services. A shared history of problem resolution and crises should be able to generate the mutual trust which would bridge ethnic, territorial and religious differences.

In the 1990s this ever-strengthening view of social development has begun to coalesce around the concept of **empowerment**. Van Eyken (1991), Friedmann (1992), Craig and Mayo (1994) and Rowlands (1997) have all examined the concept and focused on the notion of 'power', its use and its distribution as being central to any understanding of social transformation. This centrality includes power both in terms of radical change and confrontation and in the sense of the power 'to do', ' to be able' and of feeling more capable and in control of situations. Power is, in most contexts, the basis of wealth, while powerlessness is the basis of poverty and both the 'powerful' and the 'powerless' are categories of actors fundamental to understanding the dynamics of any development process. Power can be seen as an asset owned by the state or a dominant class and exercised in order to maintain its control and to stamp their authority and legitimacy. Power, furthermore, operates at many different levels and is manifest in the conflicting interests of different groups within any particular context; for example, local or regional patrons, the power that men often exercise over women and the power that institutions such as the church exercise over people. Rowlands (1997) distinguishes between 'power over', 'power to' and 'power within'; while Craig and Mayo (1994) contrast the notions of power

17

as a 'variable sum' in which the powerless can be empowered without altering the level of power already held by the powerful, with power as a 'zero sum' in which any gain in power by one group inevitably results in a reduction in the power exercised by others. Power is also related to knowledge, which is both a source of power and a means for its acquisition. In this respect it could be argued that development work is primarily to do with the control of knowledge and that if the poor were able to control the sources of knowledge, the structures of existing power relations would be radically altered. The following three quotations illustrate the range of meanings of empowerment in a development context.

. . . an alternative development involves a process of social and political empowerment whose long term objective is to rebalance the structure of power within society by making state action more accountable, strengthening the powers of civil society in the management of their own affairs and making corporate business more socially responsible. (Friedmann 1992)

Empowerment is about collective community, and ultimately class, conscientization, to critically understand reality in order to use the power which even the powerless do possess, so as to challenge the powerful and ultimately to transform that reality through conscious political struggles. (Craig and Mayo 1994)

While the empowerment approach acknowledges the importance for women of increasing their power, it seeks to identify power less in terms of domination over others and more in terms of the capacity of women to increase their self-reliance and internal strength. This is identified as the right to determine choices in life and to influence the direction of change, through ability to gain control over crucial material and non-material sources. It places less emphasis than the equity approach on increasing women's status relative to men, but seeks to empower women through the redistribution of power within, as well as between, societies. (Moser 1991)

Empowerment has become a major purpose of social development interventions in the 1990s. It has been operationalised into practical project methodologies and, in terms of its effect and impact, it is beginning to be translated into observable and measurable actions. Concretely people's empowerment can manifest itself in three broad areas: (a) power through greater confidence in one's ability to successfully undertake some form of action, (b) power in terms of increasing relations which people establish with other organisations, (c) power as a result of increasing access to economic resources, such as credit and

18

inputs. Social development as empowerment does not see poor people as deficient and needing external support; more positively, it seeks to create an interactive and sharing approach to development in which people's skills and knowledge are recognised. Empowerment is not merely therapy which makes the poor feel better about their poverty, not simply the encouraging of 'local initiatives' or making people more politically 'aware'. Similarly it does not assume that people are entirely powerless and that there do not already exist networks of solidarity and resistance through which poor people confront the forces which threaten their livelihoods. On the contrary, empowerment has to do with 'positive change' in an individual, community and structural sense, with organisation and with negotiation. But, as Rowlands (1997) has commented, 'it takes time' and is not a process that necessarily achieves results in the short term.

THE GLOBAL AGENDA

Up until the mid-1980s the notion of social development at the macro-level was largely seen in relation to other sectors and in terms of the state's role in social welfare provision. Midgley's (1995) recent summary of social development from a social welfare perspective provides both a historical and a contemporary review of this perspective and reinforces the view that, while substantial changes in the use of the term have occurred since the mid-1980s, the equating of social development solely with the delivery of social services is still strong. In the 1980s the World Bank also introduced the concept of non-economic development into its annual reports, initially in line with the notion of social welfare but later in a broader sense. The fundamental change that occurred was an inevitable recognition that development cannot be understood in purely physical or economic terms but should concern itself also with the 'development' of the people involved, not just in terms of providing them with some basic services but more substantially in terms of developing their abilities to manage, to negotiate and to advance their own development. More recently the UNDP has added the notion of 'human development' which similarly would appear to be people-centred and concerned with understanding people's development across a broad range of criteria and not the limited measurement of economic growth.

Since the mid-1980s social development has taken on a crucial role at both macro- and also more project-based development level in the face of a number of contemporary forces which are shaping the global development environment. Economic liberalisation, deregulation, privatisation, the declining role of the state and fiscal strait-jackets represent the policies and the mechanisms of the new economic order since the late 1980s and these have all helped to shape the environment in which social development will function. New policies which emphasise decentralisation, privatisation, targeting and competition have similarly begun to influence the development agenda; and new actors, such as local authorities, NGOs and private firms have all joined the process of policy formulation and taken on important operational roles. Within this changing global context, two policies in particular have had and continue to have a profound effect on the potential to promote social development:

Structural Adjustment Policies: which have been widely implemented and which have fundamentally altered the policy and resource allocation environment in which social development could be promoted. Although there was an initial assumption that the 'transaction costs' of SAPs – in both economic and social terms – would be short term, and there is evidence that they have led to more prudent fiscal management and greater market liberalisation, the overwhelming evidence is that such policies wrought substantial social havoc (Cornia et. al. 1992; Mkandawire 1994). Basic incomes of the poor have dropped, the numbers in poverty have increased, access to basic services has been severely curtailed unless cost recovery is feasible, social tensions have increased particularly in urban areas and social bonds have been broken as families – and especially women – are more concerned with coping. UNRISD (1995) reviewed the consequences of SAPs in Africa and concluded:

> In Africa the major beneficiaries of adjustment have tended to be small groups of individuals with access to foreign exchange. We are witnessing peculiar types of social polarisation and fragmentation, both of which are detrimental to the social and political order upon which independence was built.

Globalisation: the global restructuring of the institutional basis of people's livelihoods, accelerated and driven by financial flows and movements. Globalisation undermines national sovereignty, not only in economic or fiscal policy, but in the loss of social policy options in health and education. Globalisation affects national employment opportunities, dictates market formation, leads to a loss of control over national economies and encourages the spread of values and a culture which can undermine traditional patterns of social solidarity and cohesion. While global market liberalisation, economic restructuring and technological change may create substantial opportunities for some people and countries, at the same time they have contributed to increased impoverishment, inequalities, work insecurity and the erosion of established identities and values. Globalisation may generate global wealth but it also exacerbates national poverty and ushers in new social problems (e.g. drug trafficking); its technological advances can turn into a curse as they aggravate unemployment and increase exclusion; finally, it may encourage 'global enterprises' but with little notion of global solidarity (Emmerij 1996).

The dominant processes behind this drive for globalisation may now be irreversible and could be one of the factors behind the growing emergence of different forms of protest and collective action in many countries as groups, feeling threatened by processes which they cannot control, take action to secure their livelihoods (Wolfe 1996). Some groups and cultures have learned to cope, and to take advantage of the instant access to information, the many emerging global, national and regional networks and the products of the global market. Others, on the other hand, have confronted the inexorable move towards globalisation by seeking to re-assert and defend their local cultures and ethnicity. Nationalism similarly is a robust response to globalisation forces and, in the economic sphere, the emergence of regional blocs and alliances could be seen in part as a protectionist stance. The forces of globalisation are present, to differing degrees and at many levels, in most contemporary societies and constitute a backcloth against which social development will need to be negotiated.

Given the social and political turmoil and upheavals of the past decade, the social development agenda of the mid-1990s is formidable. Indeed contemporary 'social' problems challenge the assumption within development circles that the difficult issues are economic, while social policy and social problems represent the 'softer option'. In the current crisis of livelihood and civil order, the task of constructing a just, humane and productive future would appear to be a major challenge. In its presentation to the World Summit on Social Development, UNRISD (1994) underlined the key social development issues for the 1990s: (a) democracy and good government, (b) the decline of the formal sector and the increasing informalisation of labour markets, (c) the breakdown of entitlements, such as health, childcare, welfare services, (d) increasing social exclusion, (e) the increasing abuse of drugs and crime, (f) the emergence of the notion of the 'minimalist state' and (g) the interface between the weakening state and strengthening civil society. On the basis of the above key issues, UNRISD presented the following understanding of 'social development' to the World Summit:

Social development is related to economic development in that economic growth facilitates, but does not ensure, the resolution of social problems, and effective social organisation can enhance economic efficiency. Social development is more than creating 'human capital', however. It implies not only that individuals gain improved skills,increased knowledge and higher levels of well-being, but also that they enjoy equal opportunity to employ their skills productively, and a sufficient degree of economic security to make possible stability and satisfaction in their lives. Similarly, social development is related to political freedom and stability, but is more than formal constitutional democracy. Social development implies not only that people have a voice in government, but also that they enjoy certain basic human rights, that they live in equitable and just societies, that they are free to make choices in their personal lives, and that they are able to carry out their daily activities free from fear of persecution or crime.

In the context of the international framework of development assistance, the UNRISD declaration broke new ground and effectively challenged the notion of social development as social amelioration and service delivery. While it did not challenge the critical role of economic development, it argued strongly that the equality, stability and justice of the social environment in which people live is as critical, if not more, to their ability to 'develop' as is production and growth. In many ways the UNRISD declaration effectively mirrors the notions of 'empowerment' and people as being central to the development process, and it draws heavily upon broader civil society concerns with the direction of those processes. These concerns have been powerfully expressed in the notion of **social exclusion**, which has been shown to be the most disturbing phenomenon of contemporary society and one which finds expressions in all contexts as increasingly large segments of the population become economically, politically and socially alienated from the mainstream of society (Gore and Figneiredo 1996). Social exclusion results in disadvantage on a massive scale and permanent damage to the ability of entire generations to protect and to improve their life's chances.

The **World Summit for Social Development** brought together national leaders and an impressive array of representatives from civil society. Never before had so many world leaders come together '. . . to fight poverty, to create productive jobs and to strengthen the social fabric' (UN 1995). While it is reasonable to be sceptical about the potential for action and impact of such meetings, the Summit was a watershed in placing social development at the centrestage of international discussions, of legitimising its broad remit and of ensuring a yardstick against which future performance could be judged. The major outcome of the Summit was a **strategy** for the promotion of social development which consisted of four main actions.

- The Eradication of Poverty
- The Creation of an Enabling Environment for Social Development
- The Expansion of Productive Employment
- Social Integration and the Strengthening of the Social Fabric

The Summit also agreed to ten policy **commitments** to be implemented at the national and international level. These included the four main actions above, plus a call for increased resources for social development, universal and equitable access to education and primary health care and to the 'creation of an economic, political, social, cultural and legal environment that will enable people to achieve social development'. It remains to be seen what effect and impact, if any, the above ringing commitments will have on the livelihoods of the world's poor. Few social development 'workers' will base their future actions on positive assumptions concerning them. To a large extent they represent yet another list of 'good' intentions which have been a characteristic of development assistance over the past decades. Clearly the 'promoters' of social development at the rural and urban community level will not await the delivery of an environment and a commitment to social development; more probably they will concentrate on generating the public solidarity and organisation which demand them.

Box 1.2 Principles of Social Development

- that people are the reason for development and that how they are affected is the measure by which development initiatives should be judged;
- that people are the means of development; if they do not understand or are not committed to development initiatives, these initiatives will not succeed, no matter how well they are planned;
- that fair and equitable development contributes to human welfare and to the social cohesion and social stability that underpins sustainable development;
- that in a world of increasing specialisation and interdependence, new kinds of relationships, organisations and institutions will be needed if people are to benefit and if growth and development are to be sustained;
- that governments have a crucial role in shaping social policy and providing an enabling environment for poverty reduction and socially sustainable development;
- governments cannot act alone; productive partnerships between the state, the market and society are needed to foster socially sustainable development.

(Source: World Bank 1997)

23

CONCLUDING COMMENTS

The past decade has seen a major re-appraisal of the meaning and practice of social development and its broadening into a more encompassing notion of development which is 'people conscious' and concerned with improving, and in some situations radically altering, the social and political environment of poor people's lives. In more academic circles, the decade has been characterised by a supposed 'impasse' in the study of social development, as previous broad, mega explanations of development and development processes and the possibility of 'common problems' and 'common solutions' have been found wanting (Booth 1995; Gardner and Lewis 1996). Post-modernism has promoted diversity and cultural relativity and encouraged the tendency to focus on specific groups and issues with a new stress on 'bottom-up', grass-roots initiatives, which has greatly increased the significance of social development as programme and project practice and not merely national policy and social objectives. In this respect the studies of Tilakaratna (1989) and Kaplan (1996) are apposite in their respective explanations of the critical role of the 'social development worker' in promoting a more people focused and action orientated development at the grass-roots level. Furthermore the concept of social development is now being re-examined in the context of two current phenomena which add strength and vigour to its core meaning:

1. Social movements: in the light of the trends and the consequences of the neo-liberal economic agenda and the forces of globalisation, a new social order based upon networks of reciprocity, collective defences of cultural identity and other forms of coping has emerged among the groups excluded from the benefits of development (Wolfe 1996). Such movements were manifest in the developed world, for example, in the 1960s focusing on quality of life issues and anti-militarism and presenting a challenge to the dominant order of things. Social movements were also at the base of many independence struggles. While they cut across social classes, participants were mainly from the peasantry, indigenous people, workers, women and the poor. The leaders were almost always from the educated middle classes. Social action and political leadership usually integrated in the beginning, but later divided into separate entities once the nation state was established.

New social movements are often generated by uniting previously fragmented and disorganised groups around some form of external threat, sometimes with active support in the form of an NGO, which culminates in the taking of swift action to defend what are perceived as threatened common interests (Edwards and Hulme 1992). UNRISD studies in Latin America in the 1980s saw such movements as transcending strictly class interpretations of social transformation, and combining a wide range of different bases and motivations for organised action (local, ethnic, gender, regional) (Stiefel and Wolfe 1994). Booth (1995) describes such movements in India which drew large numbers of rural people, including rich, middle and poor peasants as well as landless workers. Many such movements are inspiring, confront an immediate issue, perhaps achieve a favourable resolution but are short-lived. The most enduring have proved to be those based on ethnic minorities or in situations where excluded groups are engaged in long-term struggles against a majority culture. Popple and Shaw (1997) see the role of such movements as 'a critique of the existing social order', highlighting inadequacies and offering new ways of thinking. They caution, however, that not all social movements are progressive and that they can be used to preserve positions of privilege at the expense of other groups.

This critique of the existing social order can result in new social movements seeing the older movements, particularly those of labour and class, as being part of the 'problem' and as having played a role in the formation of the values and institutions which the new movements are now acting against

2. Social capital: Putman's (1993) seminal work on Italian regional administration gave substance to the notion of social capital; that is, the will and the ability of a group of individuals or communities to live together, to cooperate and to create and to maintain for this purpose a public space of institutions, goods and services. This capital is generated by people with a shared history of resource management, problem resolution and the building of mutual trust that can transcend the many differences that can tear communities and societies apart e.g. racial, ethnic, religious and territorial. Social capital can be understood in both an aggregate sense, that is in the sense of 'public goods', such as good governance and economic growth, and in relation to a specific group of social actors. The strengthening of and respect for a nation's, community's or group's social capital can be the basis for problem and conflict resolution and can provide the mutual re-enforcing of shared values and goals. Concepts such as trust and family and cultural relations, however, vary profoundly across the globe and this diversity is crucial to understanding how social institutions function in different contexts. 'Social relations' lie at the heart of social capital analysis, in particular how the institutions of state, market and civil society relate to the household and the family and their roles in perpetuating poverty, inequality and discrimination. Essentially social capital analysis argues that social development is not simply an external construct but should be built on and seek to promote the fund of shared institutions, practices and cultural pursuits which could produce the social cohesion so dramatically lacking in many societies.

For decades in international circles social development has been employed to signify the non-economic and thus 'less important' dimensions of development. But the discourse of the mid-1990s is very different and 'social development' now appears closer to the centre-stage and faces unprecedented challenges of social disarray, social disintegration and endemic poverty. There is a sense that the tide may have turned and that purely economic and quantitative explanations of development and its outcomes will no longer suffice. In the 1990s social development has become synonymous with action for transformation and change and not merely with strategies for improvement. With this has come the urgency to better understand, track and monitor the 'progress' of dynamic social development processes, but not necessarily in the sense of formal exercises of monitoring and evaluation. This could be undertaken on three distinct but interrelated levels.

(1) On a broader, more **global** level: UNRISD (1995a) has already addressed this issue and has begun to develop a system whereby 'social progress' can be monitored and evaluated at the national level via a series of composite indicators such as 'well-being', 'human development', 'poverty improvement', employment, education, health and 'democracy'.

(2) At the **contextual** or **national** level where critical issues such as 'power', 'access' and 'differentiation' will greatly influence the social development of poor and marginalised groups.

(3) At the critical **programme** or **project** level since, without data and information from these levels, national composite indicators will be inoperable.

Progress in social development, however, cannot be understood merely as the aggregate of existing programmes and projects; it must also take into account other less project specific factors which can also be influential. Nonetheless it is legitimate, in terms of seeking to understand tangible outcomes and impact, to concentrate at the programme or project level in order to build up concrete evidence of what is happening. Social development implies social change and the challenge, therefore, is to be able to monitor, describe, interpret and ultimately evaluate this change. This book will explore this issue in subsequent chapters.

Chapter 2

Evaluating Outcomes and Impact: An Overview

It is dangerous to assume either that what has been decided will be achieved, or that what happens is what was intended. (Loasby)

INTRODUCTION

Since the late 1970s the term 'social development' has been increasingly used in the analysis of the problems of both developed and less developed countries and in strategies proposed to tackle them. While this social development was seen as having certain material or quantitative objectives, it was recognised that it also involved a range of less material and more qualitative objectives or processes which were equally critical to its effective implementation. It could be argued that it was the non-government organisations (NGOs) in the late 1970s and early 1980s who took the lead in this respect and who began to support and to promote programmes and projects which had less material and more qualitative social development objectives (Oakley and Winder 1981; Howes 1991). The 1980s saw a noticeable explosion in this type of development intervention, much of it emphasising development 'as a process' and based around objectives which contained substantial qualitative characteristics: for example, organisational development, participation, self-reliance and empowerment. The bilateral and multilateral agencies followed suit towards the end of the 1980s and it could be argued that in the mid-1990s the 'development community' as a whole has at least recognised, if not openly espoused, a broader and less predominantly quantitative understanding of social development (World Bank 1994b; Midgely 1995).

The above rapid expansion of efforts to promote social development inevitably lead to the question of how it could be **monitored and evaluated**, but to date the answer to this question has not kept pace with the ever-expanding practice. Since the mid-1980s the search has been on for an **alternative approach** to programme and project evaluation which would be more relevant and more able to capture and to understand the outcomes and impact of this practice. Essentially the issue concerns the supposed inadequacies of the 'dominant model' of evaluation in terms of the qualitative nature of social development work; the measurement of numerical values via linear 'blueprint' approaches was seen as inadequate to capture the real and potential outcomes and impact of social development programmes and projects. A key thrust of the search for an alternative has been the recognition that social development is **not** a linear and predictable process which can be understood by a supposedly causal input–output–impact relationship. Programmes and projects are the basic instruments of development intervention but we cannot base the evaluation of social development merely upon their supposed outcomes and impacts; they are not the only instruments of promoting social change (Uphoff 1989; Roche 1994). Social development has to be understood more broadly and hence explanations of its outcomes and impact have to employ a number of both qualitative and quantitative approaches and not merely seek to measure direct programme and project outcomes.

The search for a more process-orientated, qualitatively sensitive and 'learning' form of evaluation has been intense and, in theory at least, relatively successful. This search has encompassed a number of key conceptual breakthroughs each of which has contributed to the present increasingly coherent understanding of the evaluation of social development:

- illuminative evaluation (Parlett and Hamilton 1972)
- evaluation without objectives (Richards 1985)
- participatory evaluation (Feuerstein 1986)
- self-evaluation (Neggers and Wils 1987)
- qualitative evaluation (Patton 1987)
- evaluation as interpretation (Marsden and Oakley 1990)
- evaluation as critical analysis (Marsden, Oakley and Pratt 1994)
- monitoring and evaluation from a gender perspective (Walters et. al. 1995)
- individual's perceptions of change (Davies. 1995a)

Collectively the above and other works have provided the basis for much experimentation which has helped to extend interest in and knowledge of alternative approaches. They have all followed a line of enquiry which has seen monitoring and evaluation not solely from the perspectives of accountability and cost-effectiveness, but more importantly as a learning exercise and one which is negotiated and not merely imposed.

The search for the 'how' in the evaluation of social development has also been accompanied by a critical examination of the whole nature and reason for programme and project evaluation. This examination has included the question 'why evaluate?' and the answer has been largely based around issues such as 'accountability' and 'learning'. M and E are seen not as an 'end' but more as a **means** to better understand present and future quality, effectiveness and impact. To be confident of the future direction of social development initiatives, it is necessary to understand fully what has happened in the past. Furthermore there has been a widespread recognition that more formal positivistic approaches to M and E treat 'people as objects' and are out of tune with more **people-centred** development strategies which are the hallmark of the 1990s. Recent developments such as Social Analysis (ODA 1995), Social Audit (Zadek and Evans 1993) and Stakeholder Analysis (Montgomery 1995) have also all contributed to broadening the understanding and questioning of M and E. Guba and Lincoln's work on Fourth Generation Evaluation, for example, has been influential in suggesting that this new approach to evaluation 'moves beyond previously existing generations, characterised as being measurement-oriented, description-orientated and judgement-orientated, to a new level whose key dynamic is **negotiation**' (1989:8). NGOs in particular have been prodigious in examining and analysing the M and E process, particularly in terms of its purpose, its participatory focus and its critical role in assessing performance. More recently the scope of M and E has been broadened to include not only programmes and projects but also an 'organisational assessment' of the ability of the development agency to promote effective development (Fowler 1997).

There are several levels at which the M and E of social development can be undertaken; macro, institutional, strategy and micro or local. Clearly it can be argued that the M and E of any particular development intervention cannot be isolated from the wider political, institutional and cultural context in which it is being implemented. Any development intervention will both affect and be affected by these broader dimensions and these will almost certainly come out in any evaluation exercise. Indeed many NGOs are developing complex, multi-strategy programmes, linking the micro to the macro, and hence the evaluation of social development will need to take up this challenge; programmes and projects are basic tools of intervention but they must be seen as part of wider change and interventions in a particular area.

With the above in mind this chapter, and the book as a whole, will focus on **outcomes** and **impact** at the **programme** and **project level**, with the argument that, unless detailed and continuous M and E takes place at this level, it will be impossible to build up the body of knowledge which is necessary to understand the wider outcomes. The immediate project impact will be affected by other factors and issues and hence its continual monitoring should help in tracking and assessing the influence of these other forces. In this respect it would be most useful for current practice to examine some of the 'technical' aspects of the M and E of social development at the project level, but in the firm recognition that a process of M and E is not merely a question of techniques and instruments. Furthermore, any assessment of the outcome and impact of social development projects must also include an assessment of the organisation 'running' or 'managing' the project. There is a symbiotic relationship between social development agency and project and both must be included in any exercise of evaluation. It will also be important to seek out the innovative and examine alternatives to what is a dominant 'project focused, linear approach' to evaluation based on complex notions of cause and effect. We may take the project as the operational level at which to examine this complex process of outcomes and impact of social development, but we must be prepared to step outside of this paradigm if it will help us to move forward.

The purpose of this chapter is to provide an overview of the current state of play in relation to both the concept and the practice of the evaluation of social development. The chapter is based on an extensive review of documentation from a range of development agencies currently grappling with this complex process. The chapter is essentially a statement of where we were at the time of the 1996 Workshop. It does not seek to move things forward but rather to pull together current thinking and practice as a basis from which the Workshop could begin its deliberations. The chapter also is both conceptual and operational in its orientation; it seeks to explain some of the key concepts in the evaluation of social development as well as identifying some of the current major issues which appear to affect its practice.

PRESSURES TO EVALUATE EFFECT AND IMPACT

In the past five years or so there has emerged an unorchestrated chorus of demands for a better understanding of the **impact** of development interventions. This has occurred at a time when there has been an equally widespread suggestion that NGOs, for example, should seek to 'scale-up' and thus broaden the potential impact of their work (Edwards and Hulme 1992). The supposition is that all development agencies should want to increase the impact of their work in order to spend their resources in the most efficient and effective manner possible. Impact is the ultimate stage in the process of development intervention and yet it would appear that few development agencies 'last the pace' and are able to summarise, after a given period of time, what might have been the overall impact of the original intervention. In the case of NGOs, however, these demands should be seen against a background of a massive increase in funds in the past decade, but only a relatively limited investment in evaluation activities (Edwards and Hulme 1995). Furthermore, in the case of NGOs Riddell (see ODI 1996) has suggested that, in terms of evaluation, staff typically focus on what has happened over the past year, rather than on longer-term trends; and on inputs and outputs, to the exclusion of the more fundamental changes. He concludes that this practice might now be beginning to change in the face of pressure 'from above' to assess impact which, he asserts, can lead to better reports but also to exaggerated claims about their work.

These pressures to evaluate impact, which NGOs in particular seem to be under, appear to come from four broad sources:

1. In a world of decreasing funds, growing dependence upon official donors and concerns about cost-effectiveness, there are enormous pressures to monitor performance more closely and to try to document the overall impact of development work undertaken. In effect, donors want to see tangible results from their support.

2. The growing concern for 'institutional learning', to know what works and what does not and to move forward as an organisation on the basis of a continuous and systematic understanding of the effect and impact of what the organisation has set out to achieve.

3. An equal concern to ensure the 'sustainability' of programmes and projects, which can only really be assessed if there is a more complete understanding of the overall impact of the work. Sustainability implies a 'withdrawal strategy' on the part of the supporting agency and such a strategy can only be achieved if and when there is some authoritative understanding of the social development which has taken place and of its durability.

4. The increasing recognition, particularly on the part of NGOs, of the need to be accountable to the programme or project target group and the growing understanding that information on impact can have a positive effect on motivation and self-confidence.

While there have been studies recently into the impact of NGOs, 'as a species', in terms of the overall performance of the projects which they support as agencies of development, this has not proved a fruitful field of enquiry given the general poor level of programme and project evaluation (ODI 1996). A similar exercise undertaken in the context of the Finnish NGO Support Programme led to the same conclusion (Riddel et al. 1994). The crucial problem appears to lie at the level of implementation of evaluation exercises, where all development agencies face a difficult task, particularly in relation to the evaluation of qualitative change. Fowler (1997) paints a picture of the formidable theoretical and practical 'barriers' which NGOs face in identifying and measuring 'develop-

31

ment results'. The extent of these 'barriers' is perhaps borne out in a study of the Netherlands bilateral aid programme which showed that only 6% of evaluation reports were comprehensive and that most paid little attention to longer-term impact (Priester et al. 1995). ACTIONAID's current study of Participatory Impact Assessment (see Chapter 4 below) similarly points to the strength of the rhetoric in comparison to the weakness of the practice. Encouragingly, however, many NGOs and the British ODA are currently mounting exercises to examine the notion of impact and we can expect results in the near future (SCF, Oxfam/Novib, Bilance and PAC).

The crucial dimension will be impact at the programme and project level. Programmes and projects are the basic 'operational tools' and the outlet for the strategies and objectives of development agencies; it is at this level that the critical work of the M and E of 'impact' needs to be undertaken. It is only if impact evaluation work is undertaken at this level that some of the broader questions relating to, for example, 'wider social and economic impact' or 'institutional impact' can be answered. There appears to be a current dilemma in the sense that development agencies are looking to make statements on the overall impact of their work without having a detailed understanding of the outcomes and impact at the operational level. It is at this level that effective evaluation will need to be undertaken if the broader questions are to be answered. Effective M and E of the outcomes and impact of social development are also essential for predicting the future and the likely changes that could take place. M and E are essentially exercises of the past, but they are critical both for understanding the potential for future change and for institutional learning.

OUTCOMES AND IMPACT

While there may be a debate about the relevance of linear approaches to the M and E of social development, current approaches generally involve a sequence of stages, each with a series of specific tasks which must be undertaken if the desired result is to be achieved; that is an understanding of the outcomes and the impact of the programme or project being implemented. There is ample guidance in the literature, both academic and applied, on these different stages and no shortage of definitions. The more common terms used to describe these stages are: objectives, inputs, outputs, effort, effect, efficiency, effectiveness and impact. In the literature reviewed from a number of development agencies, there would appear to be a fairly widespread familiarity with the above and a number of common sources from which these agencies draw; for example, Pratt and Boyden 1985; Beaudoux et al. 1992; and Gosling and Edwards 1995. The crucial point in all of this is to get the sequence right and also to understand the relationship between the different stages. We will never be in a position to 'measure' effectively the impact of an initiative if we do not adequately complete the earlier stages of the M and E process.

In this respect the Figure 2.1 presents is a clear and useful diagram of the stages and the tasks for effective M and E. It should be borne in mind, however, that it does represent a 'blueprint' and is useful largely as a framework for reference and for ordering a sequence of actions; the crucial issue of understanding the change which might have taken place will be from the perspective of the people involved and the approach might not follow the logical sequence suggested. Furthermore, the diagram's clarity should not detract from the complexity of the relationship between the different levels. Many factors outside the project will intervene and influence changes at a higher level. It is also important to retain flexibility in our use of terms. The 'intended impact' of a programme or project is often taken to mean the longer-term, sustainable changes which it is hoped the programme or project will contribute to bringing about. But the intended 'beneficiaries' will probably judge the impact in other ways; in some situations a project may lead to changes in the shorter term which have significance for, or 'impact' on, people's lives. These may be unexpected or unintended changes, both positive and negative, arising from the project and these also should properly be described as its 'impact', whether affecting the intended beneficiaries or others.

Fowler (1997) similarly has constructed the following graphic way of understanding both the sequence and the tasks at hand in the monitoring and evaluation of development programmes and projects (see Table 2.1).

In later chapters in this book we will examine in some detail the process involved in evaluating social development in particular systems, monitoring and the selection and use of indicators. Before doing this, however, it might be use-

Table 2.1		
POINT OF MEASUREMENT	**WHAT IS MEASURED**	**INDICATORS**
Outputs	Effort	Implementation of Activities
Outcomes	Effectiveness	Use of outputs and sustained production of benefits
Impact	Change	Difference from the original problem situation

Figure 2.1

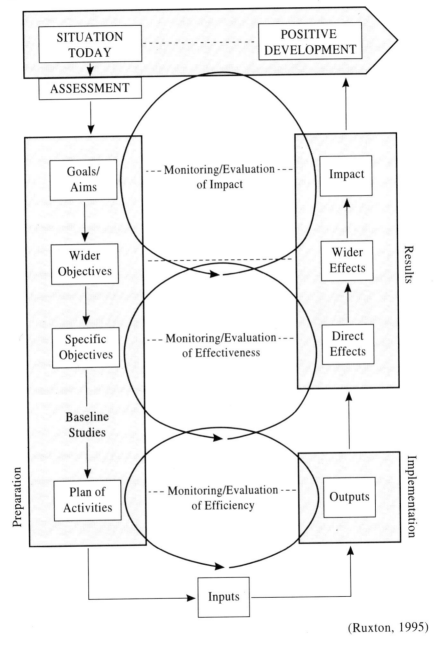

(Ruxton, 1995)

ful to examine the terms **outcomes** and **impact**. The evidence suggests that development agencies 'in general' are stronger on issues such as outputs, effort and activities, but less strong when it comes to determining what has been the result of all the endeavour. Also we should bear in mind that, while local people may be involved in definition, terms such as 'outcomes' and 'impact' often come from the perspective of donors; however, understanding the 'change' which has taken place from the perspective of the people involved will be more relevant.

Outcomes

While initially M and E will involve a detailing of effort expended and a description of activities undertaken, the crucial first stage in measurement will be to assess what has been the outcome of the project in terms of the **effect** it has had on the initial situation. In this respect, and as we have seen in Fowler's table above, there is often a confusion between 'effect' and 'effectiveness'. A project may have been 'effective' in the way it has been able to organise its inputs, deliver an appropriate service or bring about a certain change in existing practice or attitudes, but it is still necessary to understand what has been the 'effect' of all these 'effective' activities. By effect we mean the more immediate tangible and observable change, in relation to the initial situation and established objectives, which it is felt has been brought about as a direct result of project activities. This effect will need to be verifiable and 'measurable' in one form or other and it will have both qualitative as well as quantitative dimensions. Appropriate indicators will then need to be determined and operationalised in order for the effect to be observed and measured. As illustrated in Figure 2.1, which is a most useful diagrammatic representation of effect and impact within an overall project cycle, a distinction can be drawn between 'direct' and 'wider' effects (Ruxton 1995); another study has made the distinction between 'immediate' and 'sustained' effect (Valadez and Bamberger 1994). The important point to stress is that effect is more than the total sum of effort expended and the activities undertaken; it is the measurement of what all this adds up to in terms of a verifiable and potentially sustainable change in the initial situation. Finally 'effect' should not be confused with 'efficiency' – the sum of output in relation to the costs involved – which is often 'measured' in projects which involve substantial investments. However, most (smaller) development agencies are rarely able – for all too common reasons – to measure efficiency in any meaningful way.

Impact

In the overall process of M and E, **impact assessment** is the last stage and it is rarely reached. The programme or project will, of course, have had an impact but this is rarely adequately assessed (if at all) in evaluation exercises. One of the main reasons for this (among others) is that development agencies have tended to view attempts to understand the overall impact of an intervention in terms of a generalised and usually externally facilitated 'assessment' of what might have been the overall outcome, sometime after operations have ceased. In the first instance it is important not to confuse 'impact' with 'effect'; the latter refers to the more immediate outcome brought about by an intervention, the former to the longer-term change. Impact refers to the 'consequences or end products' which result, either directly or indirectly, from an intervention and on which can be placed an objective or subjective value (Lichfield 1996). Furthermore, we must also bear in mind that impact can also be negative as a result of unexpected consequences of the development intervention. It is also currently fashionable to talk of 'gender impact', 'environmental impact', 'impact on poverty', 'the impact of emergency work' in relation to programme and project operations (Hopkins 1995; DANIDA 1995). Studies often refer also to the economic, social and political dimensions of impact (Bilance 1994). Moreover, a distinction appears to have been drawn between 'impact evaluation', which is retrospective and 'impact assessment' which is predictive, although matters are at such a tentative stage that it is probably not important to be too demanding on definition. The following two statements represent the range of content and issues in this current search to understand the impact of development interventions:

Impact concerns long-term and sustainable changes introduced by a given intervention in the lives of beneficiaries. Impact can be related either to the specific objectives of an intervention or to unanticipated changes caused by an intervention; such unanticipated changes may also occur in the lives of the people not belonging to the beneficiary group. Impact can be either positive or negative, the latter being equally important to be aware of. (Blankenberg 1995a)

Impact assessment refers to an evaluation of how, and to what extent, development interventions cause sustainable changes in living conditions and behaviour of beneficiaries and the differential effects of these changes on women and men. Impact assessment also refers to an evaluation of how, and the extent to which, development interventions influence the socio-economic and political situation in a society. In addition it refers to understanding, analysing and explaining processes and problems involved in bringing about change. It involves understanding the perspectives and expectations of different stakeholders and it takes into account the socio-economic and political context in which the development interventions take place. (Hopkins 1995b)

There would appear to be very few examples of the successful evaluation of the impact of social development programmes and projects. The series of evaluations undertaken of the Finnish NGO Support Programme, for example, concluded that 'impact' was difficult to assess; the mere listing of achievements does not constitute overall impact (Bebbington et al. 1994 a and b). Squire (1994) has underlined these difficulties and suggested, for example, that the only authentic way to assess the impact of an intervention is in relation to what would have happened if the intervention had not taken place. Fowler (1997) has suggested that a major cause of the situation is the time-scale involved and the inability of development agencies to sustain evaluation throughout the whole project cycle and after. At the conclusion of Phase 1 of its PME Dialogue Process, one NGO concluded the following:

Most evaluations focus on results rather than effect and impact. There are a lot of reasons why impact is not addressed. First of all, a clear concept and definition of 'impact' is missing. Consequently, it is very difficult to work out impact indicators. Usually there is no linear or tangible relationship between project output and impact. It is much more difficult to get information on impact than on project output. It has been seen that more often process review is not being undertaken, which is an essential component of impact evaluation. (Anon. 1996)

These conclusions would seem to sum up aptly the current state of play and they constitute a challenge to development agencies. Results and output are not enough, the unpredictable process between initial input and eventual impact has to be kept as the overall framework of M and E work and the time dimension must be understood from the very beginning. But it is much more straightforward in theory than in practice.

ISSUES, PROBLEMS AND IMPASSES

A review of a wide range of development agency documentation has identified a series of issues, problems and impasses which currently appear to influence the M and E of social development. Many of these will be common currency to different staff in different agencies, but collectively they provide us with a framework for understanding some of the current concerns relating to the evaluation of social development. In this respect, and given the centrality which it has achieved in recent years, it must be emphasised that we are not talking about the extension of development impact ('scaling-up'), but about the measurement of this impact. This documentation review confirmed that there is inevitably a lag between the evolution of new approaches to M and E and their application in practice. It also confirmed an already well-known fact that the issue is not just one of 'evaluation'; the necessary **monitoring** to ensure adequate and relevant data and information for the evaluation process is the crucial first stage of the process which, if not undertaken in a relevant and systematic manner, will frustrate later attempts at evaluation.

Issues

1. The 'revolution' has taken place on paper but not yet in practice! Essentially social development cannot be measured by a simple input–output approach, although there is still great dependence on this equation. Similarly the struggle between 'control' and 'learning' continues to be evenly contested. M and E as a structured exercise remains the dominant mode, and the appetites for PME systems and instruments appear undiminished. And yet the evidence to date would appear to suggest that the M and E of social development is not a purely quantitative exercise and that less elaborate and more spontaneous approaches are needed in its monitoring and evaluation. All the literature and documentation perhaps gives a false picture of forward movement in development agencies where a substantial shift in understanding and practice of an 'alternative form' of M and E, which would be more suitable for measuring the outcome and impact of social development, would appear not yet to have taken place.

2. The evaluation of social development, by its very nature, must be based to a large extent on the interpretations and understandings of those who are directly experiencing the changes which may have taken place; an understanding of such changes is fundamental in the assessment of impact. It follows, therefore, that those whom we now tend to call **stakeholders** should be actively involved. This is not the place to debate this important issue in terms of 'scientific enquiry' as opposed to 'subjectivity', but merely to suggest that, despite clear advances, this fundamental breakthrough has not widely occurred. In an evaluation of outcome and impact there will be a number of stakeholders, both primary and secondary, who will have different relationships with the project activity which is to be evaluated: e.g. managers, trustees, donors, beneficiaries and so on. But the key and direct involvement must be at the programme and project level. If project level stakeholders are not directly involved in understanding and explaining effect and impact, then efforts to evaluate social development will be futile. This issue needs to be looked at 'in the cold light of day' and should be the starting-point from which monitoring 'systems' are set up and evaluation exercises mounted.

3. Inevitably in M and E exercises reference is made to the critical importance of a **baseline survey** (BLS), or some other form of current and retrospective information and data collection, in order to provide an understanding of the initial situation against which outcome and impact can be measured. Indeed there are a number of standard guides to what has become a routine exercise. And yet the lament on the lack of baseline information and data is quite widespread (Wils et al. 1993; Edwards and Hulme 1995; ODI 1996). In terms of social development, however, the situation is further complicated by the content of the BLS which would be required, at a later date, to evaluate such objectives as, for example, the promotion of children's rights, empowerment, the development of organisational skills, community solidarity and so on. Essentially we are talking about the need for a qualitative as well as the usual quantitative BLS and one which is related more to the expected **qualitative** outcomes and impact of the intervention. There is little evidence that this kind of qualitative BLS linked to expected outcomes and impact is presently being undertaken on any significant scale, and this is a major obstacle to the effective M and E of social development. However, Moris and Copestake's (1993) recent review of the techniques and practice of 'qualitative enquiry' provide some methodological guidance as to how such a BLS might be undertaken. To a large extent the baseline survey represents the orthodoxy of the first stage in evaluation but it is one which is beginning to be circumvented as less professionally driven approaches to assessing initial situations are being experimented with.

Problems

1. The joint issues of **time** and **timing** are problematic in the evaluation of social development. The short-term nature of much social development project funding is not well suited to the longer-term nature of the evaluation of such projects. The effect and impact of social development objectives may take much longer than anticipated; ' . . . the most important results may not be visible for two, five or even more years' (Smillie 1995). Rapid assessment or one-off structured evaluation exercises may be able to identify effect but they are generally inadequate for assessing impact. Somehow this problem will need to be overcome, but it will need foresight, a longer-term view of things and the abandoning of some well established practices to achieve this. In terms of 'timing' recent research by Oxfam and Novib has shown that, in the assessment of impact, such exercises must take place before, during and after project activities. Impact assessment should not be confined to post-project evaluation but should involve the establishing of a framework and a process of enquiry which extend throughout the life of a project and afterwards (Dawson 1995a; Wehkamp and Blankenberg 1995a). Both of these problems are well known and understood; the former is more intractable and linked to the whole donor fund-

ed project cycle, the latter is more technical and could be more effectively addressed.

2. There appears to be a tendency towards more and more sophisticated 'corporate level' Planning, Monitoring and Evaluation systems (**PME**), and yet little evidence that this initiative is resulting in more effective M and E of development projects. A review of pertinent documentation certainly suggests that agencies are keen to develop overall systems or frameworks within which M and E will take place, but that such systems and frameworks outline the structures, definition and broad principles but are less strong on operationalization. Davies (1995a) refers to what he calls the 'fate' of many M and E systems which seem to slide inevitably from 'extensive attention' to the detail of setting them up, to modest concern for data generation, to less interest in their use and ultimately to a 'minimal' interest in them as instruments of evaluation:

Table 2.2

STAGES OF DEVELOPMENT OF M and E SYSTEM	DEGREE OF ATTENTION
DESIGN	EXTENSIVE ATTENTION
IMPLEMENTATION	SUBSTANTIAL
DATA GENERATION	MORE
DATA INTERPRETATION	LESS
USE	SOME
EVALUATION	MINIMAL

The most common feature of such initiatives is the identification of 'indicators' to be used for such-and-such an objective. But there is little guidance on how these indicators are to be operationalised, what data and information are to be collected, how they will be stored and by whom, how they will then be analysed and interpreted and, finally, how the outcomes might be explained. A detailed review of the many programmes and projects it supports caused one NGO to comment: 'PME is not an end in itself. It is possible that (agencies) are making use of sophisticated PME techniques without having effective projects and development impact. This shows that there is no automatic and mechanical relationship between the sophistication of PME and the impact of development work. Thus the need is for an improved and more impact-oriented PME which does not necessarily mean more PME' (Anon.).

3. As with most evaluation work, the establishing of the **cause–effect** relationship is, by definition, particularly problematic and complicated in social development programmes and projects. As has been noted, impact is largely a function of 'change' and the qualitative change which might occur as a result of a social development intervention may not lend itself easily to ready confirmation. Change is ongoing and transitory and may be a consequence of a series of other factors. Valadez and Bamberger (1994) concluded that this cause–effect link becomes more difficult to evaluate '. . . when programs have broad objectives, such as alleviating poverty or improving the social and economic participation of women'. The difficulty is further compounded when we consider that individual agency projects can be such a small part of the overall picture as to make their association with perceived change difficult to document. Nielsen (n.d.) also argues that, since social development projects invariably evolve slowly and unpredictably in contexts which themselves are for ever changing, it becomes even more difficult to attribute cause–effect to them. This fundamental problem further underlines the critical importance of the effective monitoring of social development objectives from the beginning of the project as opposed to leaving their evaluation to the still common one-off exercise. It could be argued that efforts to establish the 'cause–effect' of social development projects (and hence the impact) are part of a desperate concern by development agencies to substantiate their effectiveness, but that it could prove to be a difficult endeavour. Indeed it could be said that proof of 'effectiveness' is not the main goal of impact assessment; it is concerned more with understanding, and learning from, the processes and approaches that have led to achieving a particular impact so that such knowledge and experience could be used in other comparable situations.

Impasses
1. M and E involves the collection, storage and eventual analysis of **data** and **information** on a particular development intervention. This is recognised practice and not in dispute, and yet it seems to be very difficult to get it right. A common observation in evaluation exercises and reviews refers to '. . . a paucity of information on how lives have been improved as a result of development interventions' (Mansfield 1996). ODI (1996), Wils et al. (1993) and Riddell et al. (1994) have all commented on the fact that the evidence (information) before them was simply not adequate enough to assess either the effect or the impact of the development initiatives which they were examining. And yet the impasse is not an absolute lack of data and information. Indeed there is talk of 'data overload' and even of 'data cemeteries'. It is more to do with the nature and quality of the information and data collected. Somehow the mould has to be broken – probably beginning with the abolition of the questionnaire! – and devel-

opment agencies need to reinterpret the entire data and information collection process. Based on work in West Africa, Dawson (1995a) has suggested that, in evaluation terms, data and information collection should concentrate on the 'most significant indicators' and thus avoid the collection of marginal or irrelevant material. 'Minimum but effective' is an often heard refrain and in this situation it would appear apt. Unless development agencies are able to pitch their data and information needs for project evaluation at a level which is both realistic (in project terms) and adequate, it is difficult to see how the above comments will not continue to be heard.

2. Similarly there has yet to be a major breakthrough in one of the central dilemmas of the evaluation of social development; namely, how to measure a **qualitative change** which is only manifest in its consequences. Brown (1994) cites the example of 'empowerment' as a qualitative change which it is difficult to 'evaluate' in its own right and suggests that '. . . it is wise to address the phenomenon obliquely rather than directly in practical evaluation work'. The objectives of social development programmes and projects are often expressed in broad qualitative terms and are simply inoperable in terms of their use in an evaluation exercise. The discourse and explanation have to come down a level and be interpreted into a series of concrete phenomena and activities which can be observed and monitored. It could be said that the whole momentum of the past decade or so in the evaluation of social development is being held back by this lack of direct experience which could show the mechanics and the operations of the M and E of qualitative change at the level at which it is occurring.

OBSERVATIONS FROM CURRENT PRACTICE

In the absence of any substantial evidence of 'where we are at the moment' in terms of the evaluation of outcomes and impact of social development at the programme and project level, the current situation is highly fragmented and does not suggest that the mould is about to be broken. Documentation reviewed on current practice prior to the Workshop fell into two broad categories:

1. Studies or statements which concluded that, for a variety of reasons, evaluations undertaken never really got past the stage of assessing the achievement of outputs and targets. Kreuse (1996) concluded as much in the context of studies on Impact Assessment of Norwegian NGOs; Mansfield (1996) made the same general observation regarding efforts to date to evaluate programmes and projects supported by SCF, particularly concerning the assessment of impact upon children; Edwards and Hulme (1992) lamented the need more generally among

NGOs for impact evaluation; and Valadez and Bamberger (1994) echoed the chorus in terms of social development programmes supported by the World Bank. Although we have no way of assessing the order of magnitude of the situation and, even taking into account the strong possibility that unrecorded experimentation is taking place in different parts of the world, there is little evidence that any substantial M and E of the outcomes and impact of social development interventions is currently taking place. This situation makes the gap which might eventually have to be leaped that much wider!

2. There is evidence, however, that a number of agencies are beginning to include notions of outcome and impact in evaluation work which they undertake, although their general conclusion is that these efforts have not been particularly successful. In his review of SCF projects, Mansfield (1996) observed that '. . . it is generally taken for granted that outputs would have a positive impact on the lives of the beneficiaries, thus making analysis impressionistic'. A Dutch Government Review (1995) of the work of the Co-financing Programme concluded that the work of the NGOs involved did have some impact '. . . albeit modest'. The substantial Impact Studies (1991 and 1994), supported by Bilance, looked at the notion of impact in an economic, political and social sense and found 'encouraging signs'. For example, in some of the 'bigger' NGOs in Asia it argued that the impact of their work is not difficult to see since the evidence was all around in the daily lives of the people.

However, even in these latter cases, the evidence was not based on hard quantitative and qualitative data and information at the project level, but much more on the experience, observations and judgement of the external consultants. Indeed in the terms of reference for one evaluation, the evaluation design did not build in any structured approach to evaluating impact but instead asked the external consultants to make some 'general observations' and 'assessment' of what they thought the impact of the project had been (Hardeman et al. 1993). In comparison with the literature of, for example, a decade ago, there has undoubtedly been a noticeable advance in terms of development agencies attempting to come to grips with notions of outcomes and impact, but this has yet to translate itself into substantial and practical guidance for how this could be achieved at the operational level.

Further to the general comments made above, a number of more specific issues were identified in the documentation which appear currently to affect efforts to evaluate social development:

• Inevitably and the perennial lament; the failure of most social development programmes and projects to adequately **monitor** activities and progress; but there are some notable exceptions (Davies 1995).

• A confusion in the use of the term 'impact'. In several evaluation studies the term 'impact' appears to be used in the sense of 'immediate outcome', or indeed it is used generally for all that happens as a result of inputs and activities in both the short and the long term (Bebbington et.al. 1994a and b).

• Many attempts at 'impact assessment' are essentially externally driven and, although 'local people' may be involved in some form of consultation, there appears to be still a noticeable reliance upon this form of 'evaluation'.

• Beware the Planning, Monitoring and Evaluation System (PME)! In both Latin America and Asia they are an emerging feature of attempts at more effective M and E, but there is evidence that they can so overwhelm in their demands that they are ineffective in practice and that '. . . old-fashioned descriptive systems are still being used' (Wils et al. 1993).

• There is disquiet in some quarters at the obligatory use of the **log frame** in formulating project proposals and in structuring the parameters, or the 'objectively verifiable indicators' against which they may eventually be judged. Despite the fact that the log frame does include wider development goals and processes, it could be argued that the log frame tends to emphasise inputs and outputs and, as a result, can act as a kind of strait-jacket for more qualitative and process related aspects of M and E.

• Encouragingly the notion of impact is being seen in the context of the overall Project Cycle and not just as an afterthought as a project draws to an end. Identification – Design – Appraisal – Implementation – Completion – and Impact Assessment are recognisable stages and, while we know that reality never proceeds as smoothly as the theory, it is indeed a substantial breakthrough if 'impact' can be built into the overall project process from the beginning and thus enable project staff to consider it at an earlier stage (Hopkins 1995b).

• References to notions of 'unexpected consequences' and 'negative impact', for example, are not uncommon in the documentation but rarely feature in the evidence presented.

Positively, however, there is now widespread recognition that the M and E of social development should be undertaken in a **participatory** manner, although the debate on the extent to which this happens in practice never ceases. Accompanying the broader promotion of people's participation in development Salmon (1989), for example, developed the notion of 'beneficiary assessment' which is a term used to describe a number of techniques to gauge beneficiary values and preferences at different points in the project cycle. This particular approach has been more favoured by multilateral development agencies – e.g. the World Bank – in their first wave of enthusiasm to involve local people in different stages of project implementation. In the 1990s the increasing use of PRA techniques has also given strength to greater local participation. Furthermore, and in recognition of the real difficulties of assessing the impact of an intervention upon a given population, there has been a limited use of 'project' and 'control' groups in the evaluation of social development. In such an approach, the control group detects and adjusts for changes which are not seen as a direct result of the project (e.g. political or climatic changes) while the project group detects both for these broader changes and for those which it feels could be directly due to the project intervention. A later analysis of the two situations at a given time should indicate the impacts which could be attributed to the project. While methodologically reference is occasionally made to this technique, there is little substantial evidence of its use in social development evaluation (Squire 1994). More recently the notion of 'participatory enquiry' has begun to be explored. Such enquiries encourage groups of local people to recall their understanding of change over a period of time and to identify what they feel are the factors which have contributed to or brought about the change.

CONCLUDING COMMENTS

Social development is neither straightforward, nor does it usually occur at a fast pace. Working with poor people who have few assets to bring about the changes that social development implies is not as uncomplicated as, for example, building a road or installing a water supply. Furthermore, predicting and measuring 'social outcomes' are not the same as achieving concrete results, and it is true to say that this continues to be the major dilemma which most development agencies face. In this respect and in the context of the particular demands made by the M and E of social development, perhaps two initial observations can be made. First, in the face of fairly widespread self-disenchantment with the current state of affairs, there would appear to be an argument for more **rigour** in evaluation procedures at the agency level. By this we mean generally more methodical, clearly defined, prompt and adequately supported M and E work, particularly at the project level. Second, the need to ensure that the **task** will be **completed**. This observation refers to the proliferation of M and E processes which outline the indicators and the 'participatory' methods to be used, but which give very little indication that these processes then complete the later stages and result in data and information on outcomes and impact. If M and E processes generally could complete their technical cycle, then perhaps we would be in a better position to judge what might have been the outcomes and impact. This technical cycle could be seen as having five interrelated but distinct stages: (a) building the framework, (b) setting up an appropriate monitoring system (c) identifying the indicators, (d) storing the information and data, and (e) analysing and interpretating. We shall look at each of these in turn in the next chapter.

Clearly what we cannot produce is a universal model of the M and E of the outcomes and impact of social development projects; social development is such a broad remit and project contexts vary to such an extent that attempting a model would be impossible. What might be useful, however, would be the construction of a broad, **reference framework** which could help in both the design and the operationalisation of social development M and E in different contexts. Such a framework would be constructed on the basis of our knowledge of the issues and of the practice to date and is already probably implicit in the many case examples which we are about to examine. However, in the construction of such a reference framework, we probably need to make two **assumptions**:

1. Agency time and resources will be in short supply, there may be significant staff mobility in terms of changes during the life of a project and that experience to date with M and E of social development will be generally limited;

2. There will be a preference for a framework which is able to deliver a **minimum but relevant** understanding of the outcomes and impact of social development, as opposed to the detailed understanding which could come from more sophisticated but also more demanding M and E systems. In other words, it will be important to pitch such a framework right and not construct a system which ultimately will be beyond the capacities of the development agency to operationalise it.

Currently both the knowledge and the practice of the M and E of social development are quite scattered and not easily available to those who work on or support such projects. Currently also the range is quite extraordinary, from approaches which differ little from essentially quantitatively orientated systems to experiments which are turning such systems upside down. In this scenario any attempt to 'pull things together' and to suggest some minimum, but proven, practices would help to consolidate a movement which is renegotiating the whole concept of project evaluation.

Chapter 3

Key Elements in the Evaluation of Outcomes and Impact

Since the recognition in the late 1980s of the critical importance of understanding and 'measuring' the changes brought about as a result of social development programmes and projects, there has been a steady and noticeable increase in the practice and the development of more qualitative approaches to monitoring and evaluation. The basis of this approach was examined at the Swansea Workshop in 1989 and subsequently published (Marsden and Oakley 1990). Since that first Workshop the emphasis has increasingly been put on the issues, problems, structures and steps involved in operationalising social development evaluation. The output of development agencies in relation to these matters has been notable, even if they have encountered enormous difficulties in the more technical aspects of project evaluation. Since the mid-1980s the practice of project evaluation has undergone a profound 'revolution' as it has encompassed more qualitative objectives and processes. There has been considerable experimentation and, as we shall see in Chapter 4, many innovative approaches. This chapter, therefore, will try to pull together what appear to be the **key elements** in this ever strengthening approach to the M and E of social development with the emphasis upon outcomes and impact. These key elements would appear to be: the overall M and E framework, operationalising outcome and impact evaluation, monitoring processes, indicators, information storage and the analysis and interpretation of data and information. This chapter will examine each of the above on the basis of the range of agency presentations at the Workshop and other literature and documentation.

THE OVERALL M AND E SYSTEM

Despite the observations made in Chapter 2 concerning the over-sophistication of monitoring and evaluation systems which some development agencies set up, the building of an overall framework of the process, stages and tasks of evaluation is a critical first step. However, the framework has got to be more

47

than a paper exercise at central level; it has to be operationalised at the project level. The lack of an overall framework can be and often is the major obstacle for initiating M and E. The 'framework' to which we are referring has several main components: structure, methods, indicators, data storage and retrieval and analysis and interpretation. Already there is evidence that development agencies are formalising these frameworks into Planning, Monitoring and Evaluation Systems (PME) which can be highly structured, not always easy to follow at a glance and begging the question of how they would be operationalised at the project level. Smillie (1995) has warned of the 'blueprint' approach to project evaluation, particularly with respect to the log frame as a means of structuring evaluation activities; and Blankenberg (1995b) refers to the genuine 'fear' on the part of NGOs that such systems might become 'top-heavy' and not justify the expenditure. However, recent developments of the notion of impact assessment in the project cycle – design, appraisal, implementation, completion and after completion – are a very useful step forward in the direction of a framework (Hopkins 1994). Essentially we are looking for some evidence of an overall 'view' of the evaluation exercise, that its various stages have been contemplated and that there is a notion that the exercise will lead to more than cataloguing effort and output. It is important to avoid situations where evaluations are undertaken as impromptu, one-off exercises with little sense of overall planning or direction. The notion of an overall framework is particularly critical in the unfolding, process nature of social development evaluation.

Increasingly, therefore, development agencies are building their project evaluation activities into institutionalised systems and moving forward on that basis. In a review in 1995, PLAN International examined the systems of a number of agencies using six key criteria: process elements, outputs, management, users, linkages and technical aspects. The review provided ample evidence of the growing tendency to build M and E into existing project planning systems and also to structure evaluation activities in a more consistent manner. There is, however, no notion of some form of universal M and E system for social development; indeed there is a remarkable range of approaches each geared to the particular nature and demands of the agency operating them. Essentially such systems follow the broad contours of the evaluation sequence which formed the basis of the case studies examined at the 1992 Amersfoort Workshop – preparation, execution, reporting and reflection – with the introduction of more formal and standard institutional principles and procedures at the different stages. The increasing interest in such systems can be attributed partly to the nature of social development. Conventional and largely quantitatively orientated evaluations are more concerned with inputs and outputs and are usually able to measure these using quantitative research methods. Social development evaluation, on the other hand, is not amenable to such limited methods and demands an approach which is more wide-ranging and capable of picking up and explaining the qualitative change which may have taken place. It is to be expected, therefore, that as development agencies – and particularly NGOs – actively promote social development in the sense that we have seen in Chapter 1, they will need to develop accordingly their M and E capabilities. There would appear to be a direct relationship between the growing influence of social development and the increasing sophistication of M and E. A detailed examination of a number of social development M and E systems reveals the following as the kinds of broad **principles** which underpin them:

- the system should be minimum but cost-effective, it should be intelligible to both staff and project partners at all levels and should not require onerous and unnecessary reporting;

- the system should be designed in such a way that it is able to develop the reflective and analytical capacities of those involved and not merely result in the mechanical undertaking of pre-programmed activities;

- the system should be able to feed consistent, quality information on output, outcome and impact into the (annual) project cycle – both for accountability and learning purposes – leading to the ongoing adaptation of plans and objectives;

- the system should emphasise decision-making and analysis and not merely be geared to the collection of information and data;

- the system should be based on the assumption that change as a result of social development may be unpredictable and that its evaluation, therefore, cannot always be based on predetermined expectations of likely outcomes;

- the system should also be based upon as wide an involvement as is realistically possible and necessary and one which values the contributions of the various stakeholder groups; it should recognise gender diversity and should seek to ensure that both women and men are able to contribute;

- the system should recognise that the most crucial aspect of the M and E of social development is monitoring and should emphasise this function as opposed to the ex-poste evaluation approach;

- finally the system should acknowledge the value of alternative sources of information, both oral and visual, and of the perceptions of local people who have not been directly involved in the project.

The above principles are, of course, far easier to express than to build into a commonly understood and used M and E system. Within most conventional understandings of a project cycle, M and E inevitably appears in the latter stages and, accordingly, is affected by the inconsistencies and difficulties of the earlier stages. Problems such as external influences, intended and unintended outcomes, the tangible and the intangible and the potentially conflicting roles of the operating agency and the donor, can all contribute to a complex and unpredictable scenario in which the system is functioning. While there would be fairly widespread recognition and solidarity with the above kinds of principles, there is little evidence that they have been widely employed in the practice of social development evaluation. Although some might argue that, by definition, such systems are anathema to social development evaluation which should be as 'unstructured' as possible, it is difficult to avoid the need for a framework which will produce, on a consistent basis, the **continuous** understanding of the unfolding process. In this respect the following are examples of social development M and E systems which were presented by a number of agencies at the Workshop.

SNV, Netherlands: PROMES (Project Monitoring and Evaluation System)

PROMES is designed to monitor and evaluate project groups and their activities, in order to facilitate activity monitoring, reporting and internal as well as external evaluation. The system focuses on the qualitative socio-political aspects of project objectives and seeks to gain information concerning the development of human resources, on changes in human relations and with the project group's position in society. Furthermore, the system is based on the assumption that community-level organisations often pursue objectives which are different than those of the project, but that the common ground are the group activities. As a result these activities are monitored by both the groups and the project staff; the group looks more at the activity–result relationship while the project staff adds to this the result–objective relationship. PROMES has been computerised and a manual on data collection has been written, thus creating a uniform system which all SNV supported projects follow. The system is based on four forms which are continuously updated by both group members and project staff:

1. Organisation: code, name, number of members (m/f), composition of committee, social linkages, age, gender and ethnic status of project group.

2. Activity: description, feasibility, beneficiaries, responsibilities of the different actors, objectives of the project, problems encountered, self-evaluation score.
3. Expenses: identification, description of project expenditure.
4. Group dynamics: indicators relating to internal organisation, outside contacts, management, gender and environmental aspects.

PROMES is essentially demand-driven and has basically been designed by staff working at the project level. It is an approach characterised by flexibility, open-endedness and 'learning by doing', which are common features of applied monitoring systems. SNV reports that, because the system is computerised, it is a powerful tool for analysis and reporting; it is easy and simple to operate and its information is readily accessible. Contrary to most M and E systems, PROMES is essentially a qualitative system and does not gather much quantitative data; its emphasis is on the 'social' effects of development projects and the changes that occur, in organisational and group relationship terms, as a result of a project intervention.

PROSHIKA, Bangladesh: Internal Impact M and E System (IIME)
Proshika, a Bangladeshi NGO which works on poverty alleviation, improving women's status, environmental protection and people's participation, lays great emphasis on an internal Management Information System (MIS) which is the basis for a range of monitoring activities designed to better track the development initiatives which it supports. Within this overall system, the IIME seeks to measure the impact of Proshika's work in two areas: economic empowerment and social empowerment. Economic empowerment is measured by a set of indicators built around issues such as income, employment and levels of indebtedness; while social empowerment is tracked by indicators such as improved social status, relations with local authorities, increase in power and the development of local capacities. Overall the IIME is divided into three sub-systems:

1. Impact Assessment System(IAS): which is based on a large-scale cross-sectional survey which is used to assess the impact of Proshika's interventions on the socio-economic profile of project beneficiaries. The household is the unit of analysis of the IAS and impact is assessed every third year.

2. Internal Periodic Monitoring System (IPMS): the sub-system tracks and monitors the progress of groups including members of the respective groups. The group is the unit of analysis within this sub-system and impact is assessed on an annual basis.

3. Sectoral Evaluation and Process Documentation: since the IPMS and the IAS are basically quantitative approaches which used structured questionnaires, this sub-system uses different qualitative techniques in order to monitor the non-material aspects of social development.

The Proshika M and E system is a detailed and highly developed one which uses well-tested social survey methods and techniques and which would appear to be consistent with the size and breadth of the operations of the organisation. Proshika's field of activities is immense and its emphasis on the economic and income-generating aspects of empowerment demand a detailed and quantitative understanding of outcomes and impact. It is a system which, while encouraging the participation of project beneficiaries in monitoring and building assessment around their responses to detailed questionnaires, also contains a strong professional element and demands fairly sophisticated levels of data collection and storage.

Lutheran World Federation: Planning and Monitoring System (PMS)

The PMS is a 'standardised' system which was set up by LWF in the early 1990s to meet four specific needs: better programme planning and management, a 'longer-term' perspective, fuller documentation and an improved basis for project evaluation. The system is expected to generate the level of detail and information which is appropriate to LWF's capacity and needs and, in this way, to strike a balance between what it calls the bureaucratic requirements of government departments and the *ad hoc* more informal approach associated with NGOs. The PMS is seen not only as a process but also in terms of a final product. It is a compulsory requirement at the LWF field office level and involves a series of clearly laid out steps leading to the creation of two common products; a field office planning document and annual monitoring reports. PMS is part of LWF's standard planning cycle of seven stages and involves inputs from a wide range of LWF staff and stakeholders at different levels. The PMS is based on three sets of documents which outline the system to be followed at the field office level:

1. PMS Planning Document: This document is divided into 12 sections or chapters which are intended to follow a logical sequence and provide a full description of the project. It is expected that field office staff will consult widely in the preparation of the project plan.

2. Annual Monitoring Reports: Produced annually and expected to reflect changes, new targets and achievements; there is, however, the proviso that as annual reports are considered inadequate, then more regular reports can

be presented. Essentially these annual reports detail target achievement and provide a narrative summary.

3. Progress Indicators: Four main types of indicators are suggested; input, output, effect, and impact, and more than a hundred specimen indicators in seven project areas are listed. There are, however, no examples to guide staff in the use of these indicators.

The above PMS is typical of the type of system which has been set up by development agencies with multiple field offices, intensive common project activities and an emphasis on financial accountability. The system is comprehensive and demanding and is intended to ensure effective control of field level operations. It is also openly biased towards the quantitative; indeed its instructions caution against the use of qualitative indicators which do not provide 'objective evidence of progress'. In this respect the system would have difficulties in effectively monitoring the true nature of social development projects.

DFID (formerly ODA): Output to Purpose Reviews (OPR)

DFID's overall M and E system has five main components: project reporting, project monitoring, project reviews, project completion reports and ex-poste evaluations. Within this overall system the log frame is the key tool both for project cycle Management and also for the assessment of effect and impact. Since 1992 the OPR has come to be seen as a key element in this overall system and as important to strengthening DFID's understanding of progress and changes at the project level. An OPR is a periodic review of an ongoing project focusing on progress at the purpose level and the causal links from output to purpose; other impacts and unintended effects are also considered. It also involves a series of people, including DFID staff, project implementers and key stakeholders, and has four key purposes.

1. To provide a strategic overview of the general direction of the project.
2. To assess progress (impact and achievements) towards objectives (purpose and goal).
3. To reassess assumptions and risks.
4. To provide recommendations and agree the way forward for the project.

An OPR is undertaken using the project log frame as the basic tool for analysis and for assessing progress; the project purpose as stated in the LF serves as the yardstick against which to judge output. An OPR should be a dynamic and interactive process between the concerned and interested parties, both ensuring accountability to stakeholders and also providing DFID with the project level information critical for assessing the overall effectiveness of its aid programme. The focus of an OPR is on both 'evolving outcomes' and 'early impact' and its task is to agree and to record progress in these two areas. An OPR is also concerned to identify lessons to be learned from the project and any 'unexpected spin-offs' from the project's activities. OPRs are particularly relevant to what DFID calls 'process projects' in which, although the goal and the purpose may be fixed, outputs can be periodically assessed for their relevance and adjustments made. Typically OPRs can be timely interventions in the project cycle and can suggest the modifications that might be useful and the actions which will need to be undertaken if a project is to achieve its expected effect and impact.

The above examples of M and E systems could be seen as a response to the limitations and the problems often associated with monitoring at the project level; inconsistency, information overload, poor stakeholder involvement, lack of analysis, bias towards the quantifiable, inflexibility and irrelevant indicators. On the basis of the evidence, it could be argued that none of the above systems appears to be able to adequately address these problems. Crucially such systems need to effectively undertake two tasks: (a) the integration of monitoring activities into the routine of project management in a functional and supportive manner, and (b) the capturing of both expected and unexpected outcomes and impact at the project level. PME systems are useful in that they can provide an overall framework within which project progress can be assessed and they offer the potential for both consistency and comparative data and information. The principle of such systems is sound but the difficulties associated with their implementation in the unpredictable world of development projects, and in particular their propensity to generate surplus demands and responsibilities often negate their effectiveness.

BUILDING IN OUTCOMES AND IMPACT

In Chapter 2 we examined the terms 'outcomes' and 'impact' as well as the emerging interest in 'impact assessment' which has begun to take on a substantial presence in the practice of the M and E of social development. The timing is apposite since a review of several studies and other documentation concluded that few evaluation exercises get past the stage of assessing the achievement of outputs and targets. Kreuse (1996), Mansfield (1996) and Valadez and Bamberger (1994) all commented, in their respective studies, on the dearth of impact assessment in the evaluation exercises which they reviewed. Indeed, Mansfield observed that '. . . it is generally taken for granted that outputs would have a positive impact on the lives of the beneficiaries, thus making analysis impressionistic'. Furthermore, there is little evidence in the literature and practice that development agencies are making the distinction between 'effect' and 'impact' in the general course of evaluation exercises and that, while they may be identified, indicators are rarely consistently monitored and measured. While these are no models in this respect and each project will by definition have to construct its own approach to impact assessment, there are a number of current examples which illustrate how different development agencies have sought to build the notion of 'impact' evaluation into their M and E work. These examples suggest a set of general principles which could be relevant in this respect.

In the first instance, Biekart's (Workshop Paper 13) work on assessing the impact of private aid interventions aimed at strengthening political roles in civil society, is useful in suggesting a number of factors which could influence design and operationalisation:

- Determining the **context** of the impact assessment. In other words, what is the basis of the assessment (e.g. project activities), the process elements in the project, the donor–partners relationship, and so on. This will be an important first step and should help to give an initial focus to the monitoring.

- **Level and target**. In other words, the impact on whom or what and at what level. These could range from the macro-political and economic, to micro-level organisational change, communities or individual households. Both levels are relevant and indeed are interrelated, but there is great potential for confusion if both levels are included within the same exercise. Where a project is overtly directed towards change at the macro-level, then focusing the impact assessment at that level is appropriate; but where it is essentially concerned with micro-level changes, it may be wiser to concentrate at that level and extrapolate upwards if that is realistic.

- Determining the central **input–outcome** (cause–effect) which is to be assessed. In other words, whose impact or the impact of what. While, of course, this relationship is entirely problematic – given the potential for external influence and the dynamic nature of social change – it will still be necessary to identify the key input(s) which are expected to cause the intended impact. By doing this, the task of identifying appropriate indicators will be made more practicable.

- The importance of building a **time-scale** into the expected impact assessment exercise. Impact is not something which occurs abruptly, but more commonly it unfolds and is unpredictable. A time-scale will need to determine when the expected changes are to be monitored and for how long; and it will also be critical in assessing the sustainability of the changes.

• The effect of **external influences** on any process of impact assessment. As is widely understood, it will be impossible to assume that it is only the project intervention and its activities which will influence outcome; at both the project and the wider context level, a whole range of unanticipated variables can potentially influence the outcome of the project.

• In cases where the intention is to assess the impact of an intervention, a policy or a relationship on a wider basis, the selection of appropriate examples and situations will be important for purposes of **generalisation**. Often the wish is to assess policy or programme impact. In these instances the selection of a representative sample of expected outcomes at different levels will need to be done with care in order that they provide evidence substantial enough to make an assessment.

More generally the World Bank's (1996) work and many other studies (e.g. Walters et al. 1995) in this field have shown that the evaluation of outcomes and impact must reflect the **perspective** of the project's **stakeholders** if is to be authentic and meaningful. While the inclusion of this dimension will inevitably make the evaluation process somewhat more complex and resource-demanding, it will help to validate the process and to bring a richness of information which would otherwise be missed by more conventional evaluation approaches. The active involvement of stakeholders is, in a sense, a matter of who defines the questions to be asked and whose perspective counts.

Another piece of ongoing research suggests that a project's **impact** could be understood as a series of **outputs** and **effects** (outcomes) which occur at different times and which accumulatively cause some noticeable and lasting change in the project's environment and in the livelihoods of the people who have been involved (DFID 1997). It is important at the beginning of a project intervention to understand this process and to be prepared to monitor the unfolding sequence of events. Effect and impact do not, for example, occur at once, thus demanding some kind of one-off snapshot of the situation; instead they will unfold in stages and, if sustainable, will increase in both intensity and extent. It would be useful, therefore, to build this notion of the 'unfolding' impact into project M and E design, to work on the basis of a series of key stages over a broad time frame and to structure an understanding of the impact within them. In this research in western India project impact was assessed by considering local perceptions of project-induced changes, in the wider context of changes occurring over the four-year period in which the project had been operating. During that four-year period the impact was assessed in relation to the unfolding nature of the project and to the different phases of project activities and inputs. This approach led to impact being understood as occurring over time and as moving from preliminary to secondary to long term. The diagrammatic representation of this unfolding impact can be seen in Figure 3.1.

Figure 3.1 shows how expected or potential impacts accrue accumulatively from project outputs over the project's life; the thick arrow indicates the progress achieved towards expected project impacts. In the initial phase of the project several preliminary impacts occur as a result of project activities (PRSs, visits, literacy classes); these include increased contact and more frequent meetings to discuss problems and potential solutions. At this stage there is no direct impact on people's livelihoods. As the project's activities develop and expand secondary impacts occur as a result of technological change; for example, a growth in assets, increased access to and availability of agricultural inputs and the adoption of more diverse varieties of seeds and crops. The improved access to resources together with links to external organisations promote new and expanded income and employment opportunities. In the long term these sets of effects increase household assets and lead to higher domestic consumption and improved productivity. The figure similarly shows that the impact from tangible technologically induced change is more immediate and visible, while intangible social and institutional changes are slower and less visible and thus more difficult to monitor. These changes include increased trust between the project and the villagers, confidence in local leaders, increased participation of women and a more even distribution of responsibilities among group members. Finally the research underlined the enormous difficulties associated with trying to determine the impact of project inputs and activities in the face of the many other variables which can affect household and institutional change at the village level. In this respect this form of diagrammatic representation is a most useful tool in monitoring these complex relationships.

The Oxfam/Novib Impact Assessment Research Programme – which is presented in more detail in Chapter 4 – began in the latter half of 1995 and examines impact not only in relation to the objectives of a specific intervention, but also in terms of the unanticipated changes which an intervention might cause. Furthermore, it is concerned with the notion of 'human development' and the impact which an intervention might have on cultural systems and the values which underpin people's lives. The research also emphasises the complex nature of social development and the need to take into account 'external factors' when seeking to assess impact. In the background documentation to the research, the following are suggested as the key principles which should underpin any approach to the assessment of impact.

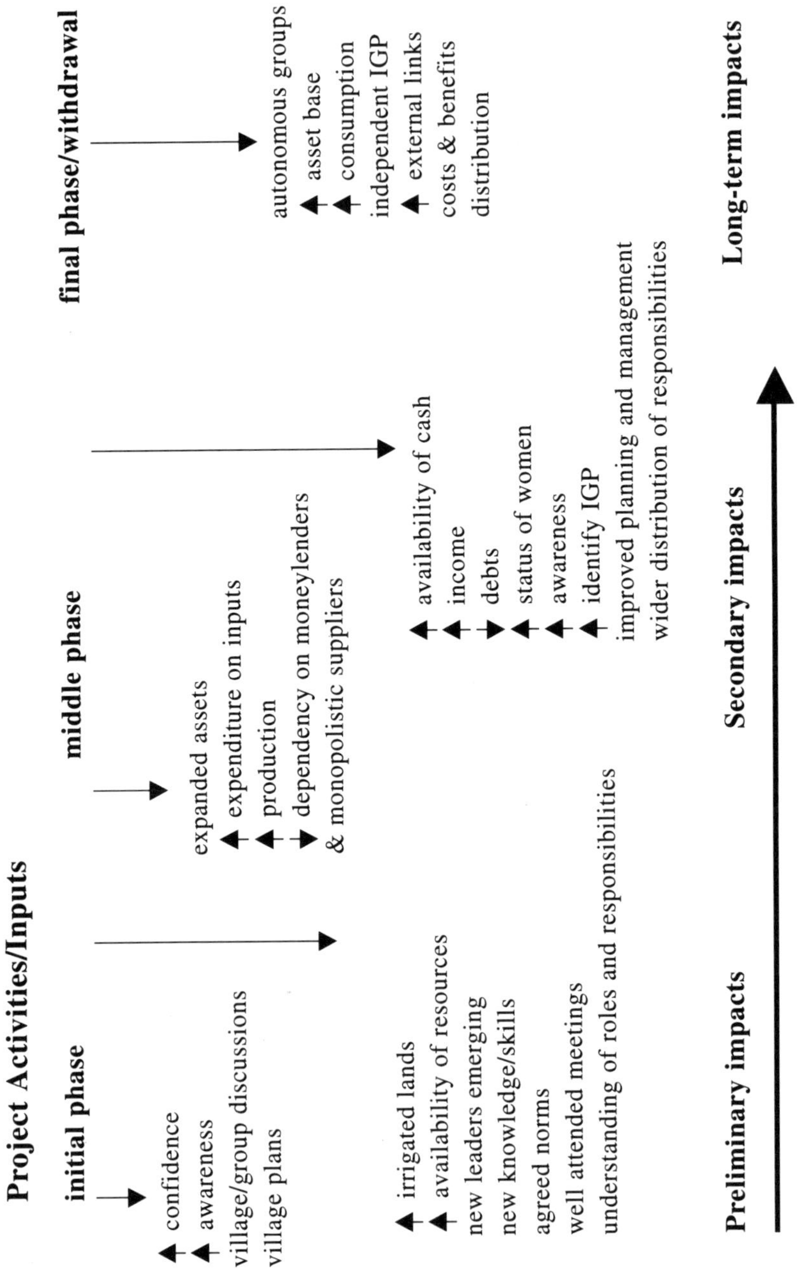

Project Activities/Inputs

initial phase

◄ confidence
◄ awareness
village/group discussions
village plans

middle phase

expanded assets
◄ expenditure on inputs
◄ production
► dependency on moneylenders
  & monopolistic suppliers

final phase/withdrawal

autonomous groups
◄ asset base
◄ consumption
independent IGP
◄ external links
costs & benefits
distribution

◄ irrigated lands
◄ availability of resources
new leaders emerging
new knowledge/skills
agreed norms
well attended meetings
understanding of roles and responsibilities

◄ availability of cash
◄ income
► debts
◄ status of women
◄ awareness
◄ identify IGP
improved planning and management
wider distribution of responsibilities

Preliminary impacts   **Secondary impacts**   **Long-term impacts**

Figure 3.1   (DFID, 1997)

- Systems need to be in place to involve stakeholders, from project planning through to the final assessment of impact.
- There should be a shared understanding of the project's aims and objectives on the part of beneficiaries, counterparts and field staff.
- Impact can best be assessed by reference to a starting-point; this might be a baseline at the beginning of a project or a retrospective reconstruction of project history and context.
- Monitoring systems should be comprehensive and track not only inputs and outputs, but also outcomes and impact.
- Monitoring of the wider environment in which the project operates is critical in order to learn about changes which can affect the project's development and the effects which a project has beyond the main beneficiaries.
- Systems for recording and reporting are required so that impact assessment in the long term can take account of progress and difficulties confronted during the project and changes in the wider environment.

It would appear also that a number of development agencies are beginning to get involved in the notion of **wider impact study** (WID) – which focus upon five core impact areas: economic, socio-cultural, capacity and power, environmental and technological (Wardle 1996). Similar to the Oxfam/Novib study, the WID approach locates impact within the broader picture of contextual change and in relation to the impact caused by the presence of long-term development programmes and not just as a direct result of project activities. The WID approach is supposedly highly participatory, with stakeholders' perceptions of change central to the assessment of impact. It seeks also to detect and to describe the causal relationship between the intervention and the changes which may have occurred. In this and in other experiments which are taking place the fundamental issue is that, in order to move beyond input and output, notions of the effect and impact of a project intervention must be built into a M and E system from the beginning. At present the evidence suggests that this rarely happens and the explanation would seem to lie in the lack of an overall M and E structure and the inability both to understand the 'unfolding' nature of impact (and to a lesser extent of effect) and to design a monitoring system which takes these two key elements on board. Furthermore, there now appears to be a fairly widespread acceptance that local women's and men's direct involvement and own perceptions, both of what constitutes change and of the nature and extent of the change which may have taken place, are crucial to the impact assessment process (Lefevre and Garcia 1997).

MONITORING

Monitoring is the more critical element in the M and E of social development, and inadequate monitoring is invariably the explanation as to why a particular project is not able to be 'evaluated' in any meaningful way. It is indeed quite remarkable, given the number of texts and guides available on project monitoring, why, in so many instances, monitoring does not take place. Essentially the reason lies in the failure to observe one or both of the two basic principles of so-called monitoring systems: (a) that they should be an **integral** part of project management and the responsibility of a special monitoring unit, and (b) that the monitoring should be seen as a structured and **continuous** process for collecting, storing, analysing and using data and information and not something which is done periodically in an *ad hoc* manner. While evaluation may well involve an external input, monitoring is normally an internal project responsibility. The major task which the M and E of social development confronts is the operationalisation of the above two principles and the acceptance by development agencies that they must be built into whatever monitoring system is set up at the project level. It is on this question that development agencies also need to discriminate more clearly between what we could term 'conventional' monitoring practice and more recent and innovative approaches. These can be distinguished as follows:

1. The first could be called the orthodox or **blueprint** approach which many development agencies have traditionally followed. A detailed monitoring system, including the selection of indicators, is set up before the implementation of the project and serves as the basis of monitoring for its duration. Such an approach could be said to have a 'control' function in terms of future reporting demands and invariably serves the needs of and satisfies donors. As is clearly evident, while this approach may be adequate for monitoring the physical input and output of projects, it can have major limitations when trying to monitor the broader, more qualitative objectives of social development, given its often inflexible and exclusive nature.

2. The second, more recent and innovative approach to monitoring, is a **process** approach and is theoretically more flexible and adaptable. This approach does not define all the key elements in the monitoring system at the start of a project; instead the system as such develops and evolves out of the ongoing experience of implementing the project. In this innovative approach stakeholders, and particularly the primary ones, have a key role since they are not used simply as the objects of exercises seeking to verify quantitative change, but more importantly they themselves suggest and describe the changes which may have taken

place. Furthermore, a process approach will also continually examine the assumptions on which the project was based and change track accordingly, and not merely crunch out the numbers. In a process approach the use of informal (often oral) information is important, since it is quicker and can often influence day-to-day decisions.

In terms of monitoring systems, the distinction between the two approaches can best be understood as follows (Marsden and Oakley 1990):

TANGIBLE OUTCOMES >>>>>>>>>>>>>>>>> **QUANTITATIVE**
(Measurement)   **(Judgement)**

PROCESSES OF CHANGE >>>>>>>>>>>>>>>> **QUALITATIVE**
(Description)   **(Interpretation)**

The monitoring of quantitative data and information is standard practice among development agencies and there are ample texts which lay out systems for these tasks and suggest how measurement can be undertaken (Clayton and Petry 1983; Casley and Kumar 1987). The monitoring of the changes associated with social development, while containing quantitative aspects, will be more dependent on the tracking of qualitative process, which will basically be done by description. This approach has led to a need for a fundamental rethink of monitoring systems so that they are able to collect, store and ultimately interpret the processes of change which have taken place.

Monitoring systems basically serve to **collect** data, information and description related to a project's progress, performance and impact. There is no shortage of guides on the range of methods that can be used in terms of a process approach to monitoring social development. For example, Valadez and Bamberger (1994), Gosling and Edwards (1995), Blankenberg (1995b) and Edwards (1996) have produced comprehensive lists, examples and discussions of the methods which can be employed for both quantitative and qualitative information: documentation review, surveys, focus groups, oral histories and the range of techniques associated with PRA. The use of such methods will be amply illustrated in the following chapter which examines a number of case studies of the evaluation of social development. Collectively these methods have helped to break the mould of more formal and disciplined approaches to data and information collection, and have encouraged the use of methods which are more consistent with people's involvement in monitoring processes and more sensitive to tracking qualitative change.

In terms of tracking qualitative change, however, the critical issue becomes one of **how much** description to include. As noted above, the description of events and phenomena over time is the major focus of monitoring the qualitative aspects of social development; indeed H. Richards (1985) argues that description is evaluation. The content of the description will, of course, be determined by which, and how many, indicators are used and this we shall examine in the next section. The crucial issue is to strike a balance between generating too much or too little description. The former can be overwhelming and the later insufficient for drawing conclusions as to outcome and impact. In this matter there are no universal rules; it would appear that trial and error and certainly experience help in determining the minimum but realistic amount of description, taking into account, for example, factors such as staff time and availability and cost-effectiveness which would produce adequate evidence for the purposes of evaluation. In relation to how much description, Walters (Workshop Paper 19) also refers to the importance of 'limiting' the monitoring system and of restricting it to the minimum set of information needed. A minimum but effective system has more chance of actually functioning than a demanding and information-hungry one.

Bergdall emphasises stakeholder participation at all levels in the monitoring process and calls for 'creative ways' of involving them in a practical way and not just as respondents to external questions (see Chapter 4.5). This demand is beginning to be heard as the evidence mounts of increasing efforts to break away from traditional, controlled monitoring systems and to experiment with approaches which are much more relevant to social development. Essentially the change is in response to the argument that **people's perceptions and experiences** must lie at the heart of efforts to evaluate qualitative change and project impact. The fundamental building-block of current efforts to develop a framework for impact assessment is the systematic involvement of local people in identifying changes which are occurring and in understanding their impact and significance (Newens and Roche Workshop Paper 44). Understanding sustainable changes in people's lives must take account of their values and priorities; projects cannot be deemed to have positively affected the lives of local people if the perceptions of the local people diverge seriously from those of external people. In certain circumstances this may mean the deliberate playing down of the kinds of data and information which formal evaluations usually value and putting more emphasis on people's ideas on the changes which have occurred. Monitoring may be a formal process, but local people also continually monitor events and change in their particular way.

Davies (1995) has done pioneering work in developing an approach to **participatory monitoring** which involves the deliberate abandonment of the use of externally determined indicators, a central concept in orthodox approaches to monitoring. The development of the monitoring system was based on the work of the Christian Commission for Development in Bangladesh (CCDB), an NGO

Box 3.1 Description as Reconstructing Project History

The broad objectives of social development projects are often expressed in terms such as 'strengthening the position of women' or 'improving the living conditions of the poor'. Though such objectives indicate in very general terms what the development agency wants to achieve, they are often inadequate for assessing impact. More operational objectives will be required and these can be reconstructed by analysing reports and by talking with people who played a role in the initial stages of the project. Information from different sources, sometimes collected through focus group discussions, may provide a fairly accurate picture, though it may not be possible to retrieve all the details. There may also be written materials available which can help to reconstruct the history, for example government statistics. For complicated and sensitive issues such as land ownership, income patterns and gender relations, it may be necessary to complement available statistics with the opinions of various stakeholders. Even more difficult are matters relating to information on and changes in attitudes and behaviour. In such cases, oral testimonies will be most useful although they may have to be supplemented with anthropological fieldwork. Impact assessment, which is based on reconstructing history, will always be descriptive and interpretative and hence raises problems between fact and fiction. Such an approach is useful and valid even if all gaps will not be filled with authoritative information and detail. In such situations 'educated guesses' and 'appropriate imprecision' are acceptable substitutes.

(Source: Es, Neggers and Blankenberg, Workshop Paper 44 1996)

with an annual budget of US$4 million. The CCDB's work takes in over 750 villages and affects some 48,000 people, of whom about 80% are women. Development assistance is in three forms; group-based savings and credit facilities, grant assistance to the most needy and skills training. The large-scale and open-ended nature of the activities pose a major problem for the design of any system intended to monitor process and outcome. The monitoring process which was tested and developed consisted of a series of steps:

Step 1: The Selection of Domains to be Monitored
　　　　Changes in people's lives
　　　　Changes in people's participation
　　　　Changes in the sustainability of people's institutions and their activities

Step 2: Establishing the Reporting Period
    To ensure that the frequency was consistent with staff time
Step 3: The Participants in the Monitoring System
    Local people, project staff, senior staff and CCDB donors; the structure of the participation would determine how the information would be analysed
Step 4: Phrasing the Question
    The basis of the Monitoring System was a simple question: During the last month, in your opinion, what do you think were the most significant changes that took place in the lives of the people participating in the project
    Respondents answered the question in two ways: (i) a description of what they felt had happened and (ii) an explanation of the importance of the changes
Step 5: Structuring the Participation in the Monitoring System
    The internal Reporting System from project office upwards to CCDB and the interpretation of information collected (see below)
Step 6: Feedback
    As each months changes were evaluated, there was a slow but extensive dialogue up and down the CCDB hierarchy as an interpretative framework emerged
Step 7: Verification
    Visits to the project site as a kind of 'policing' function to ensure that staff are kept honest in their report writing
Step 8: Quantification
    In the descriptive aspects of the system, quantitative information will be included; furthermore the numbers of changes, as well as their nature, are recorded
Step 9: Monitoring the Monitoring System
    Continually assessing and functioning of the system and its utility in relation to the task

The monitoring system as described above is both qualitative and quantitative in its approach to information collection. It is strong on the analysis of qualitative data and it is ongoing and participatory as opposed to static. The approach suggests that a key issue in the evaluation of social development is 'intersubjectivity', the extent to which different observers of events or phenomena agree or disagree with each other. Furthermore, it highlights the critical importance of 'perceptions' of change and the need to build into monitoring possible differences in these perceptions on the part of different stakeholders. It also underlines the difficulties associated with the processing of qualitative data and how to represent it in terms of how it illustrates the changes which may have taken place. The maintenance and the 'monitoring' of the monitoring system become part of the overall task in order to ensure that it continues to be relevant and consistent in the data and information which it collects.

In the development of appropriate monitoring systems for social development, Newens and Roche (Workshop Paper 44) suggest that there are a number of key 'imperatives' which should underpin this work.

- Value ongoing processes and seek information from those who are already monitoring things in their own way.
- Make information useful and relevant to beneficiaries, partners and staff.
- Develop gender and socially sensitive systems.
- Develop a shared understanding of aims and objectives.
- Develop relevant baseline data.

Newens and Roche's 'imperatives' encapsulate current concerns and thinking about such monitoring systems. Orthodox approaches to monitoring still dominate the practice and, where such systems exist, they 'play the numbers game' and seek to record inputs, quantify outputs and justify expenditure. Currently it would appear that, in social development terms, we are in a period of experimentation and evolution of more people friendly and more qualitatively orientated, but quite complex monitoring systems at the project level. The bases of the evolving system are **perception, experience** and **proximity** as increasingly it is being argued that monitoring systems are not some external, professional monopoly but that they can only be relevant if conceived, made sensitive to and developed within the immediate context of the development activity. It is possible that this current experimentation will begin to move us away from the notion of a 'monitoring system' and to structure ways in which change, in relation to a project intervention, can be understood without the recourse to formalisation. For example, ETC (Workshop Paper 28) has used 'oral histories' as a basis to understanding how people perceive the changes which have gone on and which may be continuing around them. Given the inherent instability and unpredictability of development projects, there is also a premium on the use of 'quick and dirty' methods and to approaches which ensure that 'trends' or changes are picked up and explained quickly, even if not entirely accurately, in order that they should not be lost as more formal systems click slowly into gear.

INDICATORS

A major operational breakthrough of the past decade has been development agencies' increasing familiarity with and apparent use of qualitative indicators in the evaluation of social development. The amount of discussion and examples in the literature on this matter is a reflection of this breakthrough. In this respect, therefore, there is no need to review here either the background information concerning qualitative indicators or indeed the basic issues relating to indicators such as definition, characteristics, selection and use. There is ample background material on these issues in works such as Casley and Kumar (1987), Pratt and Boyden (1985), Oakley (1988), Marsden and Oakley (1990), Westendorff and Ghai (1993), World Bank (1994b) and Gosling and Edwards (1995). The basic principles that indicators should be unambiguous, consistent, specific, sensitive and easy to collect are as valid today as they were when first suggested by Casley and Kumar in 1987. Moreover, indicators should reflect project results at three levels: **output, outcome** and **impact**; and in the evaluation of social development almost certainly both **quantitative** and **qualitative** indicators will be needed. Finally, come the questions of **who** will identify the indicators and **when**. An initial general observation which could be made would argue that while there is an increasing familiarity with the 'language' of indicators and reference to them in project documentation, there is still a predominance of indicators which show material results whereas, in the unfolding of a social development project, results are not usually predictable beforehand.

In terms of indicators of social development, the three current **key issues** would appear to be: (a) the identification and operationalisation of indicators of both immediate outcome and longer-term impact of social development, (b) research which would help us to answer the question 'how many indicators', and (c) how to develop a set of indicators that satisfies a variety of stakeholders. As regards the first, it is probably true, but challengable, to say that 'output indicators' still dominate social development monitoring activities and that 'outcome' and 'impact' indicators are still largely at the experimentation stage with, however, an increasing number of notable exceptions. Effect and impact indicators present particular problems. In the first instance, the two terms are often used interchangeably and the distinction is not made between 'effect' and 'impact'; in such cases, the use of 'impact' is more common, with the distinction perhaps being made between 'immediate' and 'long-term' impact. In this respect it is wise not to be too concerned about the correctness in the use of terms, but to stress the 'evolving' nature of overall project outcome and at least to make a distinction and to select indicators which will help to give an understanding of what is happening at two distinct phases in the project's evolution. However, there must be an intermediate stage between input and overall impact; to try to develop indicators for such a broad time span will make it impossible to identify and describe the changes as they happen. Indicators of social development, therefore, need to be selected and operationalised within the following broad framework and sequence:

**Overall >> Project >> Project >> Indicators >> Indicators of >> Indicators
Goal   Objectives Activities of Output   Immediate   of Impact
                                              and Verifiable
                                              Outcome**

While there is nothing particularly novel about the above sequence and its inter-relationships, it is remarkable how few approaches to evaluating social development seem to build around the above framework. In this sequence it is also important to stress that, as a project moves from inputs to effect to impact, the influence of non-project factors becomes increasingly felt thus making it more difficult for the indicators selected to 'measure' change brought about by the project. This fact should temper the exercise and not lead to fruitless endeavours to identify changes to reflect the chosen indicator. Second, impact can take an unexpected amount of time to occur and be evident, thus straining the usefulness of indicators to capture this change. Third, the whole exercise could be costly and time consuming, which could make it impossible for many resource-poor projects to undertake. There is no readily available empirically based evidence to provide insights into these dilemmas. Hopefully some of the ongoing enquiry into impact assessment might shed some light.

Following on from the issues raised above, an equally critical question concerns the **number of indicators** which a project might need in order for it to be able to measure the effect and impact of its activities. In this respect Carvalho and White's (1995) insistence that '. . . any list of indicators must be parsimonious and must be related clearly to need . . .' is apposite and echoed by Dawson (1995a). Similarly a review of Impact Evaluation undertaken by PAC (1995) concluded that more thought needs to be given to the number of indicators often proposed for impact measurement. This is a most crucial point since it would appear that project staff often respond to the challenge of evaluation by exaggerating the number of indicators, without taking into account the demands of their operationalisation. Certainly the literature has more than one example of lists of indicators which would appear inappropriate to the resources available. Davies (1995a), writing in the context of the Bangladeshi NGO Proshika, for example, reported on 13 indicators of empowerment which resulted in some 25 pages of questions in an evaluation proposal to measure its impact. In general terms it is wiser to attempt to assess effect and impact with a smaller number of relevant and manageable indicators, which offer the prospect of some understanding of the change which has taken place, than to be overwhelmed methodologically and timewise by an unmanageable and ambitious list.

Essentially the number of indicators used should decline as the project moves from input – output – outcome – impact. If the selection of the output indicators has followed the usual cautions about relevance and usability (and so on), they should be the basis for one or two broader indicators of outcome and then a general indicator of impact. The Impact Indicator is a 'framework' indicator and will itself need to be broken down into a small number of more specific indicators as signs increase of the impact of the intervention. For example, if we take the objective of a hypothetical social development project below, we could construct the following set of manageable indicators:

Table 3.1

Objective	Output Indicators	Outcome Indicators	Impact Indicator
Organisational development at the community level	a. Organisation formation and structuring b. Capacity building related to organisational growth c. Type and frequency of organisation activities d. Actions planned and executed	a. Emergence and strengthening of community level b. Growing involvement of the organisation in local development matters	a. Consolidation of autonomous organisations involved in local development matters

The key lesson is to keep the number of indicators down to a minimum but adequate level. It is far more effective to be able to manage and produce results from a smaller number of indictors than to be overwhelmed by an ambitious, but ultimately unmanageable, lengthy list. Data and information from the above output indicators should not be unduly complicated to collect, but do require consistency and an adequate means of storage. If those indicators begin to yield the expected information, they should provide the basis for assessing the effect and so on. It is, of course, all easier on paper than in practice and the M and E of social development, because of its more demanding and particular nature, is more prone to fall foul of the inevitable inconsistencies of development projects.

An understanding of where we are with this issue of indicators of social development is scattered across a diffuse body of documentation and literature, and synthesis is difficult. It is quite clear that, while some development agencies have yet to move beyond the discourse and a general understanding of the issues, others are not only experimenting but also seeking to draw some lessons from this experimentation. For example, several development agencies have identified and are beginning to operationalise appropriate indicators for social development. There is certainly no shortage of examples of indicators which agencies are using to monitor and ultimately evaluate the outcomes and impact of their social development projects. The following will give a flavour of the substantial progress to date of developing indicators in particular areas:

- Community organisation, poverty and knowledge transfer (Van Roosmalen and Guimaraes 1995)
- Self-management, problem-solving ability, democratisation, and self-reliance as phenomena of empowerment (Shetty 1994)
- Awareness building and access to services (Franco et al. 1993)
- Strengthening of partner organisations and stimulation of co-operation (Priester et al. 1995)
- Attitude change (H. Richards 1985)
- Autonomy, membership, knowledge base and broadening the base (Uphoff 1989)
- Access, participation and mobility of women, marriage, decision-making, awareness, self-esteem and group development (CARE 1994)

Box 3.2 Impact Indicators

- Ownership, security and distribution and security of productive assets; land livestock, labour, cash, income, and skills, especially among the very poor
- Capacity of poor people to organise themselves for collective or individual action, make claims on government and other resources and do more things for themselves more effectively
- People's self-confidence and values, on their relationships with each other, and in particular on patterns of discrimination according to gender, caste, age or other factors
- Policies and practice of development institutions, such as government, local and national, other NGOs and official agencies

(Source: Edwards 1996)

Indeed such is the proliferation of available indicators of social development that Khan (1994) has suggested that we could now group them into **generic indicator groups**. Khan equates social development with 'people learning to change their behaviour' and with 'institution building', and suggests a series of generic quantitative and qualitative indicators which should be able to monitor a number of changes over time: recruitment into programme (enrolment), continuing interest (attendance), gain new knowledge and skills (learning) and change behaviour (adoption).

This and other similar examples are now fairly common in the literature; what is less common is evidence on how the use of these indicators has worked out in practice. This is where the breakthrough needs to occur. It would appear that at the project level there are examples of experiments with the operationalisation of the above kinds of indicators, but this is not widespread and many projects probably have not moved beyond the stage of indicator identification. The key issue with indicators which have a substantial qualitative dimension is their **operationalisation** which has a series of steps beginning with their translation into recognisable and verifiable phenomena or actions which can be monitored. The overall process can be understood as below and needs to be followed in sequence if the indicators are to yield the information required in order to understand progress and change.

Selection > **Activities** > **Identi-** > **Contin-** > **Adjust-** > **Info.** > **Interpre-** > Use
of   **ication**   **uous**   **ment**   **Storage** **tation**   **Learn**
Indicators   **of**   **Monit-**   **of**   **and**
                              Verifiable **oring** **Indicators**   **Analysis**
                              Activities
                              and Actions

It is with the latter stages that the breakthrough would appear to be needed. There is still a noticeable tendency to believe that the task has been completed once the indicators have been selected; and yet, in reality, the task is only just beginning. Furthermore, these latter stages cannot be solely externally constructed and it is here that the problems are largely found. The structuring of a monitoring exercise on the lines of the above implies a more participatory and dynamic approach, one which may not be based on the conventional understanding of 'indicators' and one which will have to be very much in the hands of project level staff and local people. These latter two facts demand a design which is intelligible and workable at those levels and not simply the introduction of an externally designed system. Indeed it is the **design** of the system to apply the indicators which is key to the whole process, and we shall see a number of examples of this in the next chapter.

An area in which quite considerable experimentation has taken place is **participation** as an indicator of social development. In one sense this progress is to be expected given the fact that the notion of 'participation' is currently prominent in development thinking and practice. Works by Cohen and Uphoff (1977), Oakley (1988a and b) and Rifkin and Bichmann (1988) have been further developed by Montgomery (1995) who has summarised much of that earlier work. For example, he suggests that qualitative indicators of participation fall into three broad areas: (a) Organisational Growth, (b) Group Behaviour and Group Self-Reliance and (c) Empowerment. Montgomery's suggestion is similar to that of Khan (above) in terms of the apparent emergence of a series of generic qualitative indicators of participation, which are now quite familiar in project documentation. For instance, the Partnership Africa Canada (1995) study on impact is a useful review of similar kinds of indicators of participation; and in terms of the less complex quantitative indicators of participation, Valadez and Bamberger (1994) have usefully summarised a common set of indicators of community participation in the context of World Bank supported projects.

Reviewing the practice, there appears to be **two distinct ways** in which social development projects determine or select the 'indicators' or 'means' which they intend to use in order to monitor and assess progress and change:

1. The more common and conventional approach is that in which **indicators** are **selected** beforehand and serve as the basis for initial monitoring. The usual criteria may be applied and a list is produced. Invariably in this approach reference is made to 'participation' in indicator selection but, given the fact that the concept of an 'indicator' is probably not familiar to all stakeholders, the authenticity of many such exercises is debatable. Increasingly, however, 'participatory' indicator selection is beginning to break the mould, or at least exercises are taking place by which stakeholders might be asked how they might judge the outcomes of project activities, and their responses are then translated into 'indicators' by project management. By definition, relevant and 'monitorable' social indicators are notoriously difficult to determine, but as a fundamental principle they have to be determined within the context in which they are to operate and not be entirely external constructs.

2. In the past few years an innovative and potentially extremely influential approach has begun to take shape which eschews conventional practice in favour of the use of **open-ended question(s)** as the means for determining how progress and change are to be identified and assessed. The origin of this approach would appear to be Davies's (1995a) earlier work with the CCDB, which we have discussed above, and which is now being replicated on a minor but potentially significant scale. In place of indicators, a simple question is put

to stakeholders:
'During the past month, in your opinion, what do you think was the most
significant change that took place in the lives of the people participating
in the project?'
The potential responses to this question are then broken down into three areas:
changes in people's lives; changes in people's participation; changes in the sustainability of people's institutions and their activities.

Stakeholders' responses to the above questions are in two parts: (a) **descriptive**,
what, who, when, where and so on; and (b) **explanatory**, stakeholders' subjective assessment of the significance of the changes during the reporting period.
Both Wedgewood and Bush (Workshop Paper 22) and Bergdall (see Chapter 4.5
below) report on experiments in different contexts which have sought to apply
the above approach but we still await substantial evidence of how it works in
practice. Renshaw and Chase Smith (Workshop Paper 25) used a similar
approach in seeking to evaluate development initiatives among indigenous
people's in the Amazon region and asked key questions to do with changes in
traditional values, social solidarity and identity. This innovative approach is
technically more authentic and would appear to be highly suited to the demands
of social development evaluation. What is now needed is field evidence on how
the approach is built into monitoring systems at the project level, the reactions
and performance of stakeholders and what kinds of data and information it pro-
duces, within what time frame and how is it all managed.

A number of current initiatives by several major European NGOs in the area
of 'indicators' may well begin to alter the course of practice in the next few
years. To date the practice of social development M and E has often come
unstuck at the stage of the selection of indicators. Now these initiatives appear
to be tackling the stumbling-block head on and examining how social development process can be understood at the project level. Several established practices are up for review; for example, determining of the means to assess change,
the level at which monitoring takes place and the testing of a minimalist
approach. The emphasis on stakeholders' understanding of the changes which
have occurred is reminiscent of the 'before-and-after' approach to the description of social development which perhaps spearheaded the search for a more
effective way to monitor social development than the use of predetermined indicators. Indicators have come to be seen as 'sacred cows' of M and E; project
documents invariably include a section on 'indicators' and log frames ask for
'objectively verifiable' ones. It could be that the major practical breakthrough
in the evaluation of social development will be a relaxing of this rigid demand,
greater experimentation with more open-ended 'indicators' and the use of such
tools as 'project histories' and 'time lines' in monitoring progress and change.

Furthermore, updating indicators during the process of a project and systematic learning from the outcomes of monitoring are also key actions which would greatly enhance current practice.

COLLECTING AND STORING THE INFORMATION

We have already discussed above both the assertion that M and E systems decline progressively once they have been set up and the observation that the system often breaks down due to a lack of data and information. The collection and storage of data and information for ongoing evaluation purposes could be described as the 'engine room' of M and E; if it does not function properly, the entire system grinds to a halt. There is currently no shortage of guides to and descriptions of the range of methods of data and information collection. Valadez and Bamberger (1994) and Gosling and Edwards (1995) have produced comprehensive guides in relation to M and E; and these have been substantially reinforced by the repertoire of PRA techniques. In the past decade a whole new genre of data and information collection techniques has been developed. These eschew the more formal, quantitatively biased and discipline-based approaches in favour of techniques more suited to the demands for stakeholder participation and to the complexities of 'measuring' qualitative change. It is probably true to say, however, that their current high profile belies the situation on the ground where the collection of information is still a critical problem. Furthermore, techniques such as PRA are widely used and are strong on information collection for planning but appear less appropriate to monitoring and evaluation.

An important question to be asked in the use of the above techniques is '**how much information**' needs to be collected and recorded in order to be able adequately to assess progress. We have noted also that the M and E of the qualitative objectives of social development involves the **description** of actions and phenomena over time, and this task raises the same question. In both information collection and description, whether by using indicators or other less structured means, the issue becomes that of achieving a **balance** between being overwhelmed or not having sufficient information with which to make a judgement. There are, however, no universal rules for confronting this dilemma and it is a question of determining the minimum amount of information and description, taking into account the nature of the project and the resources available, which could produce evidence adequate for the purposes of evaluation. Perhaps the most important issue is to ensure that, at the very least, the question is addressed at the project level and that some assessment is made. Current evidence would suggest that this question is rarely asked and that little consideration is given to such issues as time, resources, staff and stakeholder familiarity and minimum

73

information requirements before an 'evaluation process' begins to function. Davies's (1995a) reference to 13 indicators and 25 pages of questions is an apposite example against which to consider these observations.

On the assumption that the above issues are being addressed, the next operational question concerns **how** the information and description are to be **organised** and **stored** for eventual analysis and interpretation. In this respect the works of Lofland (1971) on Analysing Social Settings and Patton (1987) on Qualitative Methods in Evaluation are useful texts for the general principles of practice which could be adopted. In suggesting these works, it should be noted that the context in which they are presented – education and social welfare services in the USA – is entirely different from that of a typical 'small' development project, but the basic principles which they adopt can be adapted to this latter scenario. Once the indicators (or not!), their operational characteristics and activities and methods of collection have been determined – and presumably the question of who will do all of this – then the issue of storage becomes crucial. When we ask the question 'how' the information and descriptions are to be stored, this will probably be through the use of **files** and some kind of **filing system**. Questions then arise as to the different types of file, what is to be included in the files, how often will things be filed, who will be responsible and so on. They can really only be answered in the context of a specific project when such issues as the staff resources available, staff familiarity with such techniques, timing and level of sophistication have been considered. The whole process may appear at first glance to be demanding, but if it can be pitched at the right level and be modest in its expectations, then it should be less demanding than the not infrequent excessive information demands made on field offices.

Unfortunately there are few, if any, widely available written examples of project level information storage and retrieval systems, appropriate to the qualitative needs of social development evaluation, which could provide the evidence of how such systems function and how they tackle questions like those raised above. In more quantitatively focused M and E systems, the use of computers to tackle the mountains of data is increasingly commonplace; with qualitative material the techniques are largely manual. The key features of a qualitative system are that its updating should be built into staff and stakeholders' daily activities, that it should be accessible and that it should not become a static exercise in information collection but rather a dynamic activity linked to project and institutional learning. Whatever its nature, if a system that is 'friendly' to project staff and stakeholder is not in place, the analysis and interpretation of the changes which may have occurred will be more difficult.

ANALYIS AND INTERPRETATION

The final stage of the evaluation of social development will involve the analysis and interpretation of the description and information collected. While the more quantitative dimensions of the indicators used will be measured and a numerical value attributed to the change which is seen to have taken place, analysis and interpretation are different exercises. We will need to analyse the material collected in the light of both the initial situation and the indicators used, and then to interpret the findings in terms of what they tell us about the possible change which has occurred. The purpose of the analysis is to organise the material and this will facilitate interpretation. The exercise bears some similarities to 'open-system evaluation' in that there is a continuous questioning and an attempt to understand the 'ripple effect' in terms of the impact of a development intervention. However, a 'ripple effect' does not assume that there is an automatic linear progression from output–outcome–impact; in the analysis 1 + 1 does not always add up to 2, but maybe 3 or more since there may be other unanticipated outcomes of a development intervention.

An important assumption in this process, of course, will be the existence of some understanding of the 'initial situation' against which change can be analysed. Essentially the analysis and interpretation will seek first to structure and then to provide an explicit explanation of the nature, magnitude and pattern of change which might have occurred within the given context as a result of the intervention. The key issue, therefore, is the use of qualitative indicators in the determination of what constitutes 'success' and 'failure' and the influence of language, culture and values in this process.

An examination of the still somewhat limited evidence on this latter stage of the evaluation of social development reveals a number of key practical issues. First, the potential for **subjectivity** in the description and observations made on the project and its progress and the need, therefore, to ensure that recording is structured as much as possible around the indicators, or some other proxy means. But even this may not overcome the potential problem given the inherent difficulties involved in assessing what constitutes 'change' and the fact that events and actions can be both explained and interpreted differently. Explanation and interpretation are expressions of people's values and concerns and it will be important that those of the different stakeholders are brought out and examined and compared. In this exercise Riddell's (1990) comments are apposite; '. . . if judgements made about qualitative aspects of projects are not substantially challenged by the relevant actors or groups, then purist worries about objectively assessing these factors become largely irrelevant'. Second, qualitative processes of change, by definition, can often unfold **slowly** with the result that periodically the recording might lack substance. In such circumstances there is the danger that inaccurate recordings may be made by staff anxious to see some progress. Third, the recording of description and observations can be a demanding task for which some project level workers will be more suitable than others. In the actual exercise of analysis and interpretation, there are also a number of issues which have been raised by the practice.

Firstly, the process of analysis–interpretation–subsequent action should be a participatory exercise involving both project group members and staff. The forum for the exercise is usually open discussions or review meetings, often under the guidance of a facilitator and structured around the two dimensions of the exercise and the indicators. Both individual and collective memory will be important aspects of analysis and interpretation with different stakeholders playing a role in retrospectively drawing out the major conclusions on what has been the impact of a particular intervention. This role may not come easy and it is probable that a trial period will be needed to give all stakeholders and staff the opportunity to understand the exercise and to develop the skills necessary to play an active role. Davies's (1995a) work with developing an appropriate monitoring system with CCDB explains the detail of stakeholder involvement and how descriptions of people's 'life experiences' were examined successively at different levels – project, head office and donor – and were subject to an iterated process of analysis that eventually selected a small number as illustrative of the changes which had taken place.

Secondly, analysis and interpretation should take place regularly and not be left to annual mega events. The regularity of the meetings will be dictated by factors particular to the context and to the project, but almost certainly periodic exercises of verifying what is happening will take place every three months or so. A regular three-monthly half-day exercise, which allows a project to develop an understanding of what is unfolding, is to be preferred to the annual review which can often stall at the project's inability to structure in one go all the changes which may have occurred during the year. In his approach to assessing the impact of CONCERN's work in Tanzania, Wardle (1996) underlined the importance of regular meetings, without which continuity of interpretation cannot be built up.

Thirdly, wherever possible the verbal analysis and interpretation should be translated into some kind of visual diagrammatic form. In this respect there has been a very useful development of visual techniques in the past decade and there is much with which we could experiment. In particular the range of techniques associated with PRA provides a useful base from which to start (Gosling and Edwards 1995). Similarly, Patton's (1987) concept of the Process–Outcomes Matrix offers a broad diagrammatic format within which the conclusions of the analysis and interpretation can be presented. The 'before-and-after' approach, which compares particular characteristics or actions associated with a specific indicator (e.g. group organisation) both before and after a period of project activity (Shetty 1994) is commonly employed. Another technique involves the 'spider diagram' which plots the expected changes of a number of objectives on a series of five circles spaced at fixed intervals and marks the progress of each objective on a scale of 1–5.

Finally, as the analysis and interpretation unfold over a period of time, it will be useful to begin to structure an overall framework within which the changes occurring can be located. For example, it might be possible to identify particular stages of the change taking place, which could be noted and described as a way of understanding how the change is unfolding and perhaps intensifying. In this respect Galjart and Buijs' (1982) earlier work on interpreting the different stages of the evolution of a process of participation – Mobilisation, First Action, Construction and Consolidation – provides an overall framework of stages in which this evolution could be understood. Given the difficulties inherent in determining if and when a particular stage of one of a project's objectives has been reached and what level and kind of change it might signal, projects are increasingly using numerical values and narrative to explain the unfolding process. For example, Kamara and Roche (Workshop Paper 41),

---

Table 3.2 Group Cohesion Index

0	No group, or total disintegration of an existing group.
0–1	Group formation; inactive group; group meets infrequently, does not save, no activities; high level of conflict within the group.
1–3	Normal group activities ongoing; regular group meetings, group savings, school management; resistance to individual level harassment; low to medium level conflict within group.
4–6	Group carries out activities at the village level, benefits accrue to the few rather than the collective and the action is short-lived rather than sustained.
5–8	Different groups combine together beyond the village level for a collective end and collective benefits.
8–9	A movement launched by local organisations which has a national impact and takes on the highest echelons of political power and business interests.
10	Groups of the poor take over political control at the sub-regional level.

---

reporting on an approach to measuring the unfolding level of 'group involve-ment and group identity', explain the use of an **index** as an approximate mea-sure of levels of involvement and identity within a village organisation over a period of time. This index is scored on a scale of 1–10 and is presented graph-ically as shown in Table 3.2.

Indexes, scales or other forms of diagrammatic representation of qualitative progress have been present but not widespread over the past decade and, where such techniques can be authentically used, they can be invaluable for under-standing how a particular process is unfolding. In their use, however, it has to be assumed that judgements are made on the basis of continuous and detailed recording of the evolution of the 'phenomena' under examination and that they are not the product of summary appraisals. In other words, the evidence must be available to support the progress which they suggest.

CONCLUDING COMMENTS

This chapter has suggested that a basic principle of the M and E of social devel-opment is that the approach should be 'minimal but effective'. To be effective there must be a recognisable 'system' in the sense that there is a logic, coher-ence and structure to the approach; *ad hoc*, spontaneous or discontinuous actions will not provide the consistency necessary to monitor the processes involved. However, given the nature of the processes to be monitored and the need for flexibility and adaptation, the system must neither overwhelm the actors involved nor cripple the project with its incessant demands. It is, in fact, a question of 'getting the balance right'; that is, monitoring a small but accept-able number of 'indicators', collecting the amount of data and recorded descrip-tion which is adequate to the need and building periods of analysis and inter-pretation into project activities. In all of this, it is important to take the 'broad view' by considering the exercise as a whole and to ensure that all involved have this view; otherwise the M and E can become a series of independent com-ponents, the design of each of which may not obey the overall principle. The next chapter will take us into the practice of a number of development agencies and will examine how these agencies attempt to build the elements outlined in this chapter into their monitoring and evaluation work.

Chapter 4

Examples of the Practice

INTRODUCTION

In this chapter, the experiences of five different development agencies in evaluating social development programmes are presented. These case studies were selected from among those presented at the Workshop. Each is based on experiences of these agencies' undertaking evaluations of the longer-term impact of their social development programmes. While in this chapter we include only a small number of the presentations made at the Workshop, most of the others have been included, in one form or another, in the other chapters. We think that the five presented here are the most useful in illustrating some of the major lessons, issues, principles and difficulties which these agencies have learned or encountered in carrying out impact assessment.

The contribution by Blakenberg, Newens and Roche is based on a research study on impact assessment carried out by Oxfam and Novib in conjunction with partners in nine different countries. The case study in this section focuses on five of these countries: Pakistan, India, Ghana, Uganda and El Salvador. The research has raised a number of important principles relating to carrying out impact assessment. Impact should not be assessed according to a rigid definition of what constitutes impact but rather should be guided by what the intended beneficiaries regard as meaningful to their lives. Furthermore, impact assessment needs to take account of the fact that different stakeholders may have very different views both of what has changed and how they perceive that change; impact is constituted by multiple realities, not one single reality. The research also highlighted the importance of organisational issues in understanding the impact of an agency's intervention. The case study concludes with a useful summary of practical suggestions for implementing impact assessment.

The second case study by Hugh Goyder presents the findings of the participatory impact assessment study which reviewed ACTIONAID's experiences of participatory evaluation in four different countries. The study raised a number of issues which needed to be addressed in ACTIONAID in order to improve its approach to evaluating impact. First, there is a need to use a wider variety of methods for evaluating impact. The study found that there had been an over reliance on a number of PRA methods, and that the evaluation would benefit by utilising non-PRA methods. Secondly, there had been a tendency in evaluations to underestimate the complexity of communities, especially in the analysis stage; rather than seeking convergence among different stakeholders, there is a need to recognise and respond to diversity and conflicting interests. Thirdly, while much attention was given to data collection, the analysis, storage and retrieval of information was often inadequate. Finally, too much emphasis is placed on indicators. Indicators are necessary but not sufficient in themselves. Even when indicators have been identified by beneficiaries, collecting data for indicators is no substitute for more in-depth, open-ended interaction with community members. The research showed that local communities do assess the impact of development interventions and that agencies do need to learn how to listen to and interpret their perceptions.

Michael Edward's case study looks at the experiences of Save the Children (UK) in India and Bangladesh. It is a shortened version of a much longer research report which examined the performance of two local NGOs in India (supported by SCF) and two projects implemented by SCF in Bangladesh. The study examined impact, sustainability and the cost-effectiveness of these NGOs and projects as a highly dynamic interaction of external and internal influences. In particular, the study found that internal organisational issues were crucial to successful programmes. The research used a range of methods – secondary sources, semi-structured interviews and PRA techniques – which are clearly described in the case study. The study identified six key findings concerning the NGO performance in terms of impact, sustainability and cost-effectiveness which are presented and explained here.

CINDE, a Colombian NGO, was asked to carry out an evaluation of the impact of a national education programme in Colombia; their experiences of this form the basis for the fourth case study by Maria Christina Garcia. What is of particular interest about this case study is its description of how it went about creating the data for future impact assessment using a wide variety of methods. Despite the scale of the evaluation, CINDE also learned lessons for evaluation similar to those identified in the other case studies presented here, such as the need for creative methods, involving all stakeholders, seeing evaluation as a learning exercise and using participatory approaches.

The final case study by Terry Bergdall reports on the monitoring and evaluation system used for the Community Empowerment Programme in Ethiopia. CEP has adopted a flexible adaptive approach to evaluation which is based on perceptions of change, rather than confining itself to a narrow set of predetermined indicators. The system was carefully thought out at the start of the programme and aimed to address the following questions: how to make monitoring participatory; how can stakeholders at all levels be involved; and how can information be a basis for organisational learning. Useful practical lessons can be learned from this case study through the author's description of how the monitoring and evaluation system actually operates, including how both quantitative and qualitative methods have been incorporated.

The evaluation of the longer-term impact of social development programmes is highly complex and presents challenges for which there are no easy answers. These case studies present the experiences of a number of different agencies attempting to make sense of this complexity within the constraints imposed by resources, staff skills, existing monitoring and evaluation requirements and external pressures. They illustrate genuine, innovative attempts to bring the rhetoric of evaluating impact into the reality of ongoing development programmes and should, therefore, prove invaluable lessons for other agencies grappling with similar issues and concerns.

4.1

Impact Assessment: Cutting through the Complexity

Floris Blankenberg, Margaret Newens and Chris Roche

The authors would like to thank and acknowledge the contributions of col-
leagues in CORDES, CYSD, ISODEC, Proshika, Novib and Oxfam UK/I, the
consultants and researchers who have participated, and the communities
involved in the impact assessment studies presented.

Ngos and Social Development – One Piece in the Jigsaw

Despite the complex and contingent nature of social development, NGOs need
to find practical ways of assessing the impact of what they do. This is important if we are to account to our different stakeholders for our actions and be able
to learn from our own, and others', experiences. It is also important for wider
debates about the value of aid, and the role of NGOs, in development. Oxfam
UK/I, Novib and some of their partner agencies are undertaking a joint study to
look at issues of impact assessment, trying out different approaches and tools in
a variety of situations.

The approach that NGOs take to impact assessment needs to recognise that
development is the outcome of multiple and complex change processes, and the
struggles of different interest groups, rather than a managed process undertak-
en by development agencies and NGOs through projects and programmes.
Simple models of causality, linking project inputs to outputs and impact, will be
inadequate for assessing our interventions. Rather, models are required that
embrace the wider context of influences and change processes that surround
projects and programmes, and the multifarious nature of the impact that results.

An appreciation of the complexity of the process of social development is
also influencing the ways in which NGOs are working. Many agencies, including Oxfam UK/I and Novib, are moving towards more strategic programme
approaches and recognising the limitations of discrete projects. This means that
strategies need to be developed taking account of the activities of different
actors in the development process, and seeking to collaborate with some and
influence others in order to bring about desired changes.

Impact assessment in social development is therefore multi-layered and has
multiple stakeholders. There will be those who are closest to development interventions – the intended beneficiaries (i.e. those that a project or programme
seeks to support) and the agencies contributing to a programme or project – who
have an ongoing and intimate interest in reviewing progress, learning and

adapting what is done in order to seek to maximise the impact that can be achieved in their local context. Then there will be those who are seeking to understand wider programme experiences, institutional performance and change processes, and looking for the complementarities – or lack of them – between development actors and actions, in order to develop overall agency strategy and partnerships.

Layers and Dimensions of Impact

Our working definition of impact is 'the lasting or significant changes that have occurred in the situation being assessed'. In general, we are being guided by the following considerations.

- First, different stakeholders to a development process will have different perspectives, but, in judging the impact that has resulted, particular attention should be paid to the views of those whom it is intended the intervention will support.
- Second, it is important to assess not only the intended impact of an intervention, but also unintended and unexpected changes occurring, whether these are positive or negative. These changes will affect people other than those whom it is intended the intervention will support.
- Third, amongst those whom it is intended the intervention will support, as well as amongst those beyond an intervention's focus, there will be different experiences and perceptions of the impact resulting.
- Fourth, while the intended impact of a development intervention is usually defined in relation to the longer-term, sustainable changes associated with the aims of the intervention, there may be changes in the shorter term that are attributable to the intervention and which people judge to be significant too.

While a systematic approach is useful in planning, we should be flexible in how we assess the actual impact that has occurred in order to identify the different levels of change it is hoped can be achieved. Whenever possible, in our assessment of impact, we should be guided first of all by what has meaning for the intended beneficiaries, exploring the diversity of their perceptions and experiences, but also seeking information and views from other stakeholders and considering who else might have been affected. But we need to recognise too that, with some intervention strategies, it will often not be feasible to track the impact of an agency's actions per se on the ultimate, intended beneficiaries. For instance, when agencies are trying to evaluate their advocacy work, many factors will combine in influencing the impact of a policy change on the lives of different people. Often, all that it would be practicable to do to assess the impact of an advocacy programme would be to look at whether policy changes have occurred, and to analyse the factors that have influenced this. This should not detract from a wider concern to know how people's lives are changing.

The Case Studies

Box 4.1 below describes the main case studies that will be referred to in this section. The experiences we shall share are eclectic, as we are not seeking one, ideal methodology for impact assessment. Rather, we are exploring a range of tools and approaches that can be drawn on depending on the purpose and context of any particular impact assessment. We will briefly look at some of the issues we are facing in relation to:

- overall approaches – the challenges of developing ongoing monitoring processes, reconstructing the past and special times of reflection and review;
- the need for openness and focus;
- the issue of attribution;
- the influence of development organisations;
- the evaluation of advocacy strategies and programmes.

Box 4.1 Case Studies

1. Project impact assessment in Pakistan
A tool to assess non-economic impacts is being developed and tested with a range of projects in Oxfam UK/I's programme in Pakistan. The tool encourages groups of project beneficiaries to look beyond the stated objectives of an intervention and to consider unintended and unexpected impacts as well as the intended. The tool is being developed by Sabina Alkire, a researcher.

2. Integrated rural development and tribal development programmes in Orissa, India
The Centre for Youth and Social Development (CYSD), supported by Novib, is exploring both retrospective and longitudinal approaches to assess the impact of their programmes.
- The Integrated Rural Development Programme started in 1988 and has focused on poverty reduction and alternative sources of income, building community based organisations, watershed management and sustainable agriculture. CYSD is now looking back at the impact that has resulted.
- The Integrated Tribal Development Programme concentrates on several

---

tribal communities belonging to the poorest groups in the State of Orissa. Areas of work include education, health, environment and livelihood issues, participation in local government institutions and cultural communication. CYSD is establishing a longitudinal study to assess the impact of this new programme as it progresses and contributes to future planning.

3. Institutional capacity building in Northern Ghana
The Integrated Social Development Centre (ISODEC) is carrying out an institutional capacity-building programme with members of a development network in Northern Ghana. Supported by Oxfam UK/I and others, ISODEC is exploring the impact on poverty of this capacity-building programme. The study starts from an assessment of changes that have taken place in the programme area and seeks to understand what has brought about these changes. A longitudinal study will then chart changes at an individual, community and organisational level as the programme progresses and seek to explore correlations.

4. A refugee settlement in Northern Uganda
Oxfam UK/I developed a programme to support 55,000 Sudanese refugees in Ikafe, Northern Uganda, settling them in small dispersed groups and allocating them land with the aim of developing a certain degree of self-sufficiency. Several agencies work with the refugees and there is support from a number of donors. Assessing the impact of programmes for the settlement of refugees brings into sharp focus the need to consider the perspectives of different stakeholders. The participatory review process at Ikafe sought to do this.

5. Post-conflict reconstruction in El Salvador
The Foundation for Cooperation and Community Development in El Salvador (CORDES) is an NGO created by the mandate of the communities with whom it works. These include demobilised combatants from the civil war of 1979–91 and repatriated and marginal communities from the areas most affected by the armed conflict. CORDES worked with these communities during the last years of the war and since. Projects now concentrate on agricultural production financing, marketing and institutional strengthening. Supported by Novib, CORDES is looking back to assess the impact of its work.

Note: During 1998, the learning from a wider range of case studies and ongoing programme experience will be brought together. This will include material from Bangladesh, Zimbabwe, Kenya and Peru.

Exploring Different Approaches

One aim of the Oxfam UK/I and Novib research study is to try and establish a process of participatory enquiry and monitoring from the beginning of some programmes, which will allow impact to be assessed as the programmes evolve. This approach to impact assessment is theoretically attractive as it offers the potential for addressing some of the common constraints found when impact assessment studies are done after programmes have finished: i.e. programme objectives are not clear; there is a lack of baseline data; and documentary evidence is weak. It also has the potential for encouraging a process of learning and adaptation in the light of changing circumstances and experience, putting those closest to an intervention – the intended beneficiaries and front-line programme workers – at the centre of assessing the intended and unintended impacts of a programme as it unfolds, as well as involving other stakeholders throughout the process. There are many questions to be tackled in such a longitudinal approach. What investment has to be made by different stakeholders to be involved in the process? Can the process be sustained without substantial outside facilitation and support and, if it cannot, is the approach appropriate? Can the qualitative data be captured, both for local memory and learning, and for sharing and affecting change beyond the programme's domain? These are some of the issues that we are looking at as we try and find practical approaches to strengthening local analysis and learning, in order to both understand and enhance the impact of projects and programmes.

Secondly, we are also looking at how history can be reconstructed when stakeholders do want to look back at the impact that has occurred as a result of change processes and interventions in the past. This is the situation we often face and it is an approach that lends itself to making comparisons across programmes too, so it has importance for learning about themes, overall strategies and methods. In this part of our research, we are trying to address some of the common constraints mentioned above that are often found in retrospective studies.

Thirdly, we are interested in how special times of reflection and review can complement ongoing monitoring processes and contribute to the process of impact assessment.

The Journey towards Impact

The impact assessment studies of CYSD's Integrated Tribal Development Programme in India and ISODEC's Institutional Development Programme in Northern Ghana are examples of where an ongoing process of assessment, learning and adaptation throughout the life of a programme is being established, involving different stakeholders to the planned development process. At this stage in the development of these programmes, the learning is mainly about involving stakeholders in programme planning and the establishment of baseline data.

The Integrated Tribal Development Programme decided to involve three main stakeholder groups – the intended beneficiaries, village leaders and government officials – in establishing objectives for the programme and indicators for assessing impact. Views were sought from women and men, younger and older people and other groupings within the overall population of potential beneficiaries. The issue then faced by the CYSD team was how to integrate different perceptions and opinions into a programme plan that would be acceptable to all. The team decided that CYSD had to play an important role in the interpretation of the wishes and expectations of the groups and in decision-making about the direction of the programme. In general they decided to follow the opinions of the majority of the population, but at the same time leave room for specific interests. Sometimes, the opinions of particular stakeholders had to be neglected.

From both this and the ISODEC study, some general issues emerge about the early involvement of different stakeholders in a programme's development. We have found that involving different stakeholders in analysis requires a high level of trust, and this cannot be assumed at the beginning of a programme. It also requires time and we have to consider how much time busy people are able and willing to commit, especially at the beginning when trust may not yet have been established. Then there is the issue of whose opinions gain precedence. This raises questions about both the methods used to seek people's opinions and the role of the NGO. In large community meetings, certain interest groups may dominate, and more informal ways of drawing out the views of marginalised groups are necessary. The NGO can have a powerful role in determining which interests guide the direction chosen for the programme, so its ability to recognise its own interests and biases, and to seek out and represent the views of marginalised and powerless groups, is crucial.

Creating village profiles at the beginning of the ISODEC programme has provided interesting lessons about establishing baselines. Using variants of participatory learning and action (PLA) exercises, information on ethnic and clan identities, and how they are linked to poverty and exclusion, has been obtained. Basic wealth categories within communities have been established. Within households, differential access to, and control over, resources has been explored, using an adaptation of a gender sensitive framework (the Harvard framework). These analyses provide useful information from which to assess, later on, who within communities and households is benefiting from changes taking place and how. This will be done by repeating some PLA exercises and by following a sample of individuals and households for a period of a year to assess changes in their lives. The profiles have provided the sampling frame for selecting these households and individuals, whom the research team hope to interview. The sample will emphasise poorer households and women. A balance of age groups and whether people are potential beneficiaries or not of the NGO/community based organisation projects will also be considered in the sampling.

The choice of research tools was found to require care in this study. Whatever the approach adopted in a study, keeping in mind the key questions to be answered is crucial in deciding which tools 'fit'. It was evident in some instances in this study that there was a danger of discussion about the tools dominating to such an extent that the ultimate purpose of the exercise would be forgotten. Secondly, some tools – particularly PLA tools – were found to be too complicated or have given unreliable information, and others were not found to have general enough applicability.

As well as using participatory research and survey techniques, ISODEC is collecting secondary data and a literature review has been undertaken on poverty and institutions in Northern Ghana. In this way, it is hoped that the findings of the study can be compared to, and analysed within, a broader contextual framework.

Reconstructing History

CYSD's Integrated Rural Development Programme commenced in 1988, so the impact assessment study that was started in 1996 is one that has sought to reconstruct the past and assess the changes that have occurred over time. The village profiles created at the beginning of the ISODEC programme also sought to establish changes that had occurred in the community over the past few years. Some of the questions that arise from our studies so far relate to issues of recall and analysing the impact of programme interventions in relation to wider change processes in the community.

In CYSD's programme, it was decided that the beneficiaries of the programme would be the main providers of information, although other informants and sources of data have been used to help reconstruct a fuller picture. It has been found to be important to work with beneficiaries in small groups, differentiating between women and men, younger and older people, different occupational groups and so on. Methods used have included asking simple and factual questions, visualising, drawing village maps, taking walks in the fields and story-telling about specific incidents.

The inevitable limitations in individuals' recall of information over a long time period always needs to be considered in retrospective studies. In the case of the CYSD research team, they have become aware that respondents may have a selective memory, perceptions may contradict established facts and some respondents may feel obliged to overstate the positive role of CYSD. They have therefore sought to cross-check data between respondents and supplement this data with field observations and analysis of documentary evidence.

In seeking to identify past changes in the programme communities, ISODEC has used change charts, trend analysis and other adapted PLA tools. They have worked with the communities to draw out quantified assessments of the level of some of these changes, and make rankings of their impact. The analysis has also looked at the perceived importance of government agencies and NGOs in bringing about these changes. The data gathered is interesting but, as with the CYSD programme, the research team have felt that other sources of data need to be used to cross-check the findings. For instance, the veracity of the quantitative data is doubted and, in particular, as already mentioned, in large groups there was the danger of the views of certain interest groups dominating and strong opinions being taken as the accepted view.

The CYSD research team has found that while the village residents are able to describe changes that have occurred in their environment, it is often difficult for them to think about the impact of CYSD interventions in particular within this wider context. CYSD has therefore decided that the research team needs to analyse and interpret the answers of the beneficiaries while taking account of external factors. This interpretation in turn is fed back to the beneficiaries for validation. Maintaining good rapport between programme staff and beneficiaries has therefore been identified as a critical factor in retrospective studies, if this kind of dialogue and validation of observations is going to be possible beyond the conclusion of programmes.

Times for Reflection

A review of an Oxfam UK/I programme to support refugees in Northern Uganda illustrates how an intensive period of study can complement an ongoing monitoring process. Dedicated periods of time for reflection and analysis are especially important in order to involve different stakeholders at various stages of a programme's development – during its planning, implementation and after its conclusion. In the case of the programme at Ikafe, the review mentioned here took place a year and a half after the programme started.

A review team of 17 people was brought together, involving different stakeholders – Oxfam UK/I staff, representatives of other implementing agencies, refugees and local council members. The team was facilitated by two Oxfam UK/I advisers.

The team 'brainstormed', studied secondary information, interviewed people in refugee and local Ugandan settlements and facilitated a series of meetings with various interested parties. These meetings gradually brought more and more stakeholders together. Visual techniques, such as impact diagrams, were used to organise, discuss and analyse complex data.

The study highlighted the importance of listening to different stakeholder perspectives about the impact of an intervention – in this instance, the different views of the refugees and the local host community in particular, but also the perspectives of local government officials, donors and programme staff. The importance of considering women's and men's interests and concerns separately was also evident in this situation. The programme had achieved much in accordance with the plans – for infrastructure development, food and water delivery, health and education services, allocation of land and support for agriculture, forestry and community development – and there had been benefits for the local Ugandan population as well as the refugees. What the review was able to do was to go beyond this level of analysis. It looked at what different groups thought were the important changes for them – positive and negative – both brought about by the programmes and other factors, and considered the constraints on the achievement of the programme's aims. It was important to consider many factors – environmental conditions, the security situation and donor policies, for instance – in understanding the complexity of how people's lives, opportunities and social relations had been affected.

A process of checking back on initial findings with stakeholders was an important aspect of this review process, as in the study of CYSD's Integrated Rural Development Programme. In the case of Ikafe, it brought stakeholders together to discuss the areas of constraint to achieving the programme's aims that had emerged from the review. In this way a deeper understanding and agreement about the problems and their causes was sought before recommendations were drawn up by the review team.

Especially in situations such as Ikafe, where stakeholders did hold different perspectives on what the programme could and should try to achieve, a special time of intensive review seems necessary to complement ongoing monitoring processes. But there are particular challenges in undertaking a participatory review in situations where conflicting perceptions about a programme are liable to occur. If differences between groups are to be brought into the open, careful consideration is required about the tensions that might result and the possible ways of mediating different interests.

Remaining Open and Strategic

An interesting issue, when deciding on tools to be used, is the relative merits of open participatory approaches on the one hand and on the other more focused enquiry which ensures that certain dimensions of change are explored, including the impact relating to the aims, objectives and underlying principles of the programme.

One technique being explored in the ISODEC study is to 'turn the telescope round', asking open questions about changes in the programme communities, and then seeking to identify to what those changes are attributed. Stakeholders are not asked to focus straight away on change they attribute to programme interventions. This may help reduce any tendency for programme impacts to be over-emphasised, and help identify the main factors and processes that local people feel are bringing about changes. In this study, interesting differences were found between what women and men tended to mention as important, as one might expect. In one case, women cited certain developments within the community as most important, for example the establishment of women's groups and the subsequent perception of 'women gaining more recognition from men'. Men, on the other hand, tended to focus more on services from outside the community, for example the services of the Ministries of Health and Education and the Ghana Highway Authority.

The participatory tool being developed by Sabina Alkire, and tested with Oxfam UK/I projects in Pakistan, starts with the project intervention and seeks to assess the full range of impacts attributed to it. A discussion is facilitated with groups of project beneficiaries about the impacts from the project. This may involve making an impact diagram. But, because open discussion and the creation of impact diagrams can often omit impacts which a group assumes development NGOs are not interested in, or which are temporarily forgotten in the excitement of the exercise, the tool being tried in the Pakistan study involves the asking of strategic, open-ended questions. The questions 'bring up' broad dimensions of human development – if these have not come up spontaneously – which are often valued, though very differently defined, across cultures. Having identified a full range of positive and negative impacts, the group then does a ranking of the strength of the impacts generated by the project to date. So, in one of the projects in the study, a micro-credit project for goats, which had been assessed as successful in terms of its economic impact, the women involved felt that the impact of the project on other aspects of their lives was as strong, or stronger. For instance, women valued the new decision-making powers they had gained and being able to offer a goat at Kurbani Eid.

This technique of offering groups a broad framework of dimensions, that they then define and explore from their own experience, seems to offer several benefits. It is a way of addressing the problem that communities are more likely to report impacts they think will be of interest to the NGO. It may be a starting-point for the development of participatory indicators to be monitored in the future, or for planning how the community can deepen certain positive impacts and address negative impacts. The tool might also invite consideration of issues that the NGO wishes to probe. For instance, the Oxfam staff added the category of 'gender relations', which might not have been spontaneously raised with an open approach. Finally, if the facilitator is accompanied by a discrete note-taker, this method can help the NGO to 'hear' the impacts in the words of the beneficiaries.

How the Jigsaw Fits Together

Understanding how changes are brought about, and the influence of specific interventions, is central to the concept of impact assessment, but we must beware of trying to prove definitively what is often unprovable. In the realm of social development, there is usually not one reality to be discovered, but rather multiple interpretations of reality. The proverb 'success has many parents . . . failure is an orphan' may well have the ring of truth for us as we seek to unravel what factors have had a bearing on a situation. So might one indicator of a project's success be that many people want to claim it, and an indicator of failure be that it is 'an orphan'?

Talking with different stakeholders and using different sources of information to cross-check information, are ways that have been mentioned of bringing some rigour to an analysis of qualitative changes taking place. Comparing the judgements of different 'researchers' is another way. Feeding back initial findings to stakeholders for further discussion can also lead to new interpretations and explanations. A recent impact assessment study by Proshika, in Bangladesh, illustrates how one NGO experienced the importance of combining some of these approaches. They started their study with a survey, feeding back the results to groups of beneficiaries and staff in workshops. This showed that while the survey methodology was useful for collecting data on some topics, beneficiaries and staff challenged the findings in other areas and deeper analysis of some social issues then ensued in the workshops. These, in turn, led to follow up PLA exercises on some of the topics, which led to further insights.

The approach being taken in the ISODEC study, of starting with different overall changes in a community and asking people what has brought about these changes, may help programme impact to be seen in context and analysed in relation to other change processes.

Then there is the issue of control groups, the classical method for studying causality in scientific research. This poses an enormous challenge when we are studying changes in communities and controls are seldom attempted. CYSD and CORDES were nevertheless keen to seek control communities for their studies. In the case of CYSD they have faced practical difficulties and moral dilemmas in pursuing this. Inevitably it was not possible to find identical communities and eventually they found ones which they considered were 'reasonably similar'. Especially in the case of the longitudinal impact assessment of the Integrated Tribal Development Programme, CYSD struggled with whether they could ask communities to commit time, and provide information, when they will have no involvement and no benefit from the programme being assessed. Offer of support in the future might act as an incentive, but CYSD is not in a position to be able to guarantee this. Despite these dilemmas, it has been possible for CYSD to go ahead and involve control communities.

CORDES is working in an area where there are several other agencies involved with development activities, and appreciates the difficulty of isolating the impact of their own interventions from those of the other agencies. They decided to try and establish control communities and received a positive response from those approached. They have chosen two control communities to compare with the project community. Some of the criteria used for choosing the controls were the origins and characteristics of the population, geographical zones and the number of families. The communities felt that the impact study could be of great use to them, helping them reflect on interventions in their communities and enabling them to compare themselves with others. There were other factors which encouraged the communities to want to take part in this particular instance. For instance, both communities have, or have had, contact with CORDES and Novib, and they were interested in contributing to the learning that would come from an international study. They have asked CORDES to help them integrate the results of the local study into future plans for their communities. This is being done through a diagnostic exercise as part of the study with the control communities and following this with planning workshops. Hence, gaining the cooperation of communities to participate as controls has been found to be possible in this instance too. Substantial differences are being found in the situation of the project and control communities, but it is too early to say whether the comparisons that can be made will be sufficiently rigorous to help understand which differences are linked to programme interventions.

The principle of controls can also be considered at the level of individuals within study communities. In ISODEC's study, for instance, the sample of households and individuals to be interviewed over a period of a year, in order to explore changes in their lives, will include people not involved with the NGO/CBO projects as well as potential beneficiaries. Although the sample will be small, it will add another dimension to the data that seeks to examine the influence of the projects alongside other changes.

Ultimately, whatever techniques are used for assessing the impact occurring, and its attribution, judgements are involved. We have seen that it is often project workers and local researchers who are in a pivotal position for making such judgements, comparing and contrasting information and opinions from different informants and sources of data. This may be done to assist communities to draw conclusions about individual interventions and local change processes, or to analyse data across a range of communities and projects.

One example of trying to help programme staff bring some rigour into how they make overall assessments about individual projects, and compare results across projects, is from the Pakistan study. Here a qualitative grading system was developed to assist staff to make overall judgements from the range of quantitative and qualitative data available to them about the projects, including

93

the group assessments of impact. A key principle agreed was that two or three people should do the grading, and that they should each do this independently. Transparency in how the grading was done was also accepted as another principle, with the graders deciding and documenting: (a) the categories on which impact was to be assessed and (b) the criteria for grading each variable.

Judgements are central to the process of impact assessment. The approaches and tools that have been mentioned here are some of the ways in which we can improve the quality of data available to us, and the process by which we make these judgements.

Examining Ourselves – the Influence of Development Organisations

Although reviews of evaluations continue to conclude that 'impact data is exceptionally poor', it is found that evaluations do, interestingly, analyse the perceived critical success factors for programmes and projects (OECD 1993). Institutional capacity and the competency of staff emerge as two key factors. Impact assessments therefore need to go beyond dissecting programmes and projects, considering the views of different beneficiaries and others and analysing external factors and processes. The influence of the different organisations within the aid process – the donors, intermediary agencies and local implementing agencies – also need to be considered.

The ISODEC study is therefore of interest, as a key aim of the research is to assess the impact of institutional capacity-building on poverty alleviation. Organisational self-assessments by members of the network of NGOs and CBOs have been one of the early activities of the programme. This has not only helped establish the capacity-building needs of the membership, but provides baseline data against which changes can be assessed, and will allow some correlation to be attempted between organisational changes and changes for individuals in the communities served by the projects. An open approach was adopted in these assessments, as ISODEC and Oxfam UK/I wanted to identify how people within the network organisations judged their strengths and weaknesses. It was decided not to influence the assessments by using predetermined checklists for organisational assessment. The results showed that some aspects of organisational capacity, which ISODEC and Oxfam UK/I consider important, did not emerge from the self-assessments. These differences are now being considered with the members of the organisations as the framework for capacity-building is developed, so that the objectives of the programme are determined in a participatory way. The organisational features identified by the members will be critical indicators for monitoring change, but it is important that ISODEC and Oxfam UK/I are transparent too about the indicators they think are important in assessing institutional development.

CYSD has sought to involve the communities in their programme area in assessing a specific aspect of their organisational capacity – that is, the different groups of workers initiating and leading the development activities in the community. In this initiative, as an integral component of the impact assessment study of the Integrated Rural Development Programme, members of the communities were asked to assess the village *animators,* traditional birth attendants and teachers assisting them.

A more holistic look at the influence of the different organisations in the aid chain seems still to need further exploration and is pertinent to developing stronger mutual accountability in partnership arrangements. Perhaps implementing organisations are often not inclined to look critically at their funders, given the unequal power relationship between funders and recipients. Or perhaps funders are not perceived as having an important influence. In an exercise at a Novib workshop with NGO leaders in Thailand, Venn diagrams were used to identify the important actors in the projects of the NGOs. Funders were sometimes not mentioned or were represented by small, distant circles showing their perceived limited influence. It needs all actors in the development process to collaborate in seeking to understand how, together, we are influencing the impact that is resulting for communities.

The Impact of Advocacy

Evaluating advocacy work also demands that we learn how to cut through the complexities in order to make reasoned judgements. As with any other programme, there will be a hierarchy of results that we would like to see from advocacy interventions. In general this moves through a continuum from:

- heightened awareness about an issue;
- contribution to debate;
- changed opinions;
- changed policy;
- policy change implemented;
- positive change in people's lives.

For different programmes we need to decide what it is important, practical and possible to do to assess our work. So, for instance, for a national campaign on health user fees, different levels of analysis might be possible compared to how international lobbying on the issue of debt could be assessed. While the ultimate change in people's lives is the central concern, as we move through the hierarchy, more and more factors intervene and we need to decide how far it is appropriate even to try to attribute influence.

The approach taken in two recent evaluations of advocacy in which Oxfam UK/I was involved, was to interview a range of people close to the policy-making process. For example, in an evaluation of a campaign by a group of UK-based NGOs about the level of the aid budget, face-to-face or telephone interviews were conducted with about 20 people. This provided rich information about individuals' perceptions on the efficacy of the strategies adopted in the campaign and judgements about its influence on the setting of the aid budget.

It seems that relatively simple approaches such as this can help us to learn, and begin to judge our performance in an area of NGO activity where little evaluation has been attempted.

Cutting through the Complexity

Moving from the theory to the practice of impact assessment is challenging, but we need to cut through the complexities and look for practical ways of building sufficient integrity and rigour into the approaches we adopt. Some issues and principles that we are finding useful as we try to do this are:

- Using simple methods of talking to those most closely involved in the situation being assessed – valuing their knowledge and judgements as a prime source of information.
- Cross-checking information from a range of informants and stakeholders, and seeking other sources of data for validating and looking for the wider relevance of the findings.
- Drawing from a broad range of methods, depending on the situation, in order to gather and analyse qualitative and quantitative data. Adapting tools to particular situations.
- Using methods that ensure marginalised voices are heard and the views of specific interest groups do not dominate – this often means using informal ways of talking with people in small groups or as individuals rather than emphasising formal gatherings. This is important for ensuring that, for instance, women's voices are heard.
- Capturing, and holding on to differences, rather than losing them through aggregation.
- Finding methods that will guide discussion to address key issues, such as fundamental development principles and the aims and objectives of an intervention, but which also open out, rather than restrict, the scope of the discussion of impact. 'Turning the telescope round' too and looking at all changes occurring in a community or within households, to complement more focused methods.
- Considering the part that implementing and support agencies are playing in influencing the impact occurring.
- Identifying those who are in prime positions to help make overall judgements on the impact of interventions – often 'front-line' staff or

members of the organisations engaged with programmes and projects – and encouraging the development of tools to help them use the qualitative and quantitative data available in a sufficiently rigorous way.

As other studies show (OECD 1993; Booth 1995), NGOs require a range of methods and tools to assess what they do. We need methods and tools that are appropriate to our size and the scope of our work. We need different approaches to assess different types of intervention. If we recognise that effective strategies have to include pushing for change over and above the community level, then we have to judge at what level 'results' can be assessed too. In this regard, there seems to be potential in combining community-level, participatory approaches with other methods and sources of documentary evidence. This can not only strengthen the judgements that can be made at a local level; it can also give a new dimension to conventional approaches for wider, 'macro' analysis by adding qualitative data about how individuals experience and perceive changes in their lives.

The OECD/DAC study noted the risk felt by some that increasing demands for impact assessment could alter the balance of NGO work away from the innovative and risk-taking. A proper concern with demonstrating 'results' needs to be balanced by an equal concern for learning from new and challenging situations. NGOs, like other development agencies, cannot mobilise support for processes of change solely on the basis of the justness of the cause. The moral case also rests on achieving such change. However, not publicising the fact that producing that change is unpredictable, difficult to assess and backfires from time to time, provides ammunition to critics who can influence public opinion by unearthing 'one or two "horror stories" of failed projects, or by a polemical diatribe in the fashionable language of the day' (Cassen 1994). The challenge for development agencies is not only to develop adequate methods of assessing the difference they make, but also to develop the courage to be honest about the results of those assessments and the necessary humility about their role as individual actors in the process of change.

4.2

Participatory Impact Assessment: ACTIONAID's Experience

Hugh Goyder

Background

Many development agencies find it difficult to reconcile their increasing use of participatory approaches with the requirements of formal evaluation systems. Historically this tension has been quite marked in ACTIONAID, which has tried both to have high standards of traditional accountability and to find ways of maximising participation by 'beneficiaries' at every stage of an intervention.

A common response to this tension is to make considerable use of participatory approaches in the early stages of a project, especially the appraisal and identification stages, but to revert back to more traditional, agency-led, indicators for monitoring implementation, and evaluating of the results. ACTIONAID has a standard practice of using participatory approaches in the preparation of 'Long-term Perspectives' which try to offer a long-term strategy for reducing poverty in a particular area. This involves both project staff and the people with whom they are working focusing together on long-term issues and discussing possible solutions to which both the agency and the people are prepared to contribute.

However, it has often proved difficult to sustain this level of participation when an evaluation is carried out at a later date. While most evaluations of NGO projects include some kind of interaction with 'beneficiaries' (though often of varied quality), the beneficiaries concerned normally have little control over the content of these discussions, which are therefore bound to reflect largely the priorities of the evaluation team and the agency being evaluated. A further issue is one of incentives: at the appraisal stage PRA approaches are often less familiar and there is an expectation that those who commit the time will benefit in some way from this effort. At the evaluation stage, unless an agency is planning to remain working in the same area, there is less incentive for people to participate.

The Introduction of Participatory Impact Assessment Methods in ACTIONAID

Most ACTIONAID programmes around the world have been trying out different variants of Participatory Rural Appraisal (PRA) over the last ten years. For a period at the end of the 1980s, some senior staff and trustees were interested in the agency using a number of centrally determined 'key indicators' like child mortality, child malnutrition, and literacy rates. This led to some useful internal debates in the organisation about how an international NGO should best assess its 'impact', and in particular on the extent to which this assessment could be done either on the basis of centrally determined indicators, or indicators specified by 'beneficiaries'.

It was not hard to question the validity of 'key indicators', especially the statistical indicators which were initially proposed. What has proved much more difficult, and still remains a challenge, is to identify an overall monitoring, evaluation, and impact assessment system which allows some comparisons to be made between different projects in different countries, and yet allows due account to be taken of local factors, local differences in programme design, and above all the interests and perceptions of beneficiaries themselves.

This debate encouraged the agency, in 1994, to seek funding from ODA (now DFID) for a specific research project aimed initially at the identification of impact indicators by beneficiaries themselves. A number of ACTIONAID projects in four countries (India, Bangladesh, Uganda, and Ghana) agreed to participate in this research and have continued to be involved throughout. While more informal, and less well-documented, experimentation in the use of participatory approaches continues in most ACTIONAID country programmes, this research project has enabled staff and some of the local NGOs with whom we work, to use some broadly similar approaches in some very different settings and to try to document these experiences in a comparable way, using outside consultants. Much of the material that follows is drawn from the reports by the consultants, Davies and Williamson.

Participatory Impact Assessment: The Methods Themselves

Discussions between NGO field workers and communities often tend to focus on discussions of 'problems' and possible solutions to which it is assumed, either implicitly or explicitly, the agency may contribute. Sometimes even 'participatory' exercises with communities can perpetuate traditional dependancy relationships, especially if the timing, agenda and scope of the discussions are all controlled by agency staff.

Participatory Impact Assessment (PIA) methods need to focus on peoples' longer-term experiences of change and their hopes and fears for the future. In this way an intervening agency should be able to get a far clearer view about the long-term dynamics and changes in the communities in which they are working. Although there were local variations, some broadly similar methods have been used in the four countries involved in this research using PRA techniques. The most useful included preference ranking and discussions with groups and individuals. Preference ranking involved making comparisons across people (e.g. well-being ranking), across activities (e.g. preference ranking of NGO services) and across events in time (e.g. ranking the importance of different events in a community's history). The consultants noted that

> In the ACTIONAID research preference rankings were widely used and exhibited two positive features. The task generated interest amongst the participants, and their preference rankings showed significant stability over time, suggesting the method was a reliable form of measurement. (Davies and Williamson)

A range of discussions were held, mainly in groups, but also with individuals. For instance in Ghana field staff had relied initially on group discussions as the main mechanism for interacting with communities. Through this research, and other evaluation work, it was found that the poorest individuals, and their specific needs, were being overlooked in these discussions, and the project then relied more on individual, rather than group, discussions.

In all the countries different uses were made of visualisation techniques, including use of drawings and photographs. There was a mixed experience of the impact of these techniques.

Key Lessons from ACTIONAID's Research

As always with innovation, through this project ACTIONAID has learned lessons both positive and negative. First we had not realised before undertaking this research the 'hold' which a relatively small number of PRA approaches seem to have over development workers in most countries, and the need for much greater discretion before any particular tool is used. In the light of this finding we would want any future research to focus more explicitly on a critical review of various PRA methods, with a view to establishing which are most helpful in enabling both beneficiaries and agencies understand the impact of different interventions.

In many of the project areas PRA approaches had been used before but the findings of these earlier exercises were not always referred to, suggesting a broader problem in the evaluation of social development – that often systems for the analysis, storing, and retrieval of key information are inadequate, and there is therefore a temptation for those involved in specific research or evaluation exercises to ignore all previous work. This relates to a critical problem of documentation in many projects: normally both field-workers and community members have valuable insights on impact which are excluded from any evaluation process focusing on written material.

Throughout this study we have continued to debate both the extent to which

EXAMPLES OF THE PRACTICE

participatory approaches should focus on 'indicators' as such, and also whether use of such indicators alone is likely to result in a clearer understanding of impact by poor people. The conclusion we reached was that broadly indicators are usually necessary but rarely sufficient. Thus they may be valuable as points of reference and discussions, but the choice of indicators needs to be based on a solid foundation of strong dialogue between NGO staff and their 'beneficiaries'. There is an obvious danger that if donor agencies start demanding beneficiary-determined indicators, that long lists of such indicators will substitute for the detailed and continual interaction between agency staff and communities that is the essential ingredient of PIA.

One of the worries in this research was the reliability of indicators identified by people themselves. Would people be consistent in their choice of indicators over time, or would these change, for instance according to seasons? The study found both that people were surprisingly consistent in their selection of key indicators, but if an NGO has been working in a particular area for some time it should not expect people to produce indicators very different from those it has been using itself. What is useful is a focus on the differences between both individuals and groups of people in their perceptions (which may be reflected in their choice of indicators). There is also a particular value in seeing how the indicators that particular groups of people select change over time.

Most development workers are now aware that communities are rarely homogeneous, and that participation requires a range of complex and extended consultations. All these studies involved varying degrees of differentiation of the population concerned, so that it was common to meet the different groups (men/women, young/old) separately. While the value of differentiation on the basis of gender should be self-evident, there may be dangers in this approach if the staff involved start from an assumption that men and women have different interests defined by their gender roles. Hence, they start with an implicit assumption that men and women are going to give priority to different indicators.

There are numerous other ways of differentiating communities on the basis of age, caste, wealth status or location. The difficulty ACTIONAID has experienced is that we found it easier to set up participatory exercises with a wide range of people in a community than to interpret and analyse the data collected by these means. Once a mass of evidence has been collected, there is a temptation to look for some type of 'convergence' between the interests of the different groups, rather than to welcome and explore the key differences between them. In the case, for instance, of ACTIONAID-Uganda a strategy of aiming to work through Parish Development Committees led the agency to identify interventions on which there was likely to be maximum overall agreement.

There is a further difficulty in analysing the data produced by research work of this type. If some analysis is attempted, it is not always easy to convert it into interventions which are substantially different from what might have gone ahead even without detailed and time-consuming discussions. We often under-estimate the time required by PRA work, and we therefore need to be more cer-tain that the extra knowledge gained by these approaches is worth the time people have to commit. We need to ask ourselves more often 'what do we real-ly need to know'; and what is the most efficient method of collecting this infor-mation.

We tend to assume that these participatory approaches (and the time they take) are 'empowering' in themselves, but the evidence on this from our study is not conclusive. The more that people can see real changes in their situations as a result of their own 'participation' the greater the sense of empowerment, but if nothing changes people may become sceptical over time.

An important conclusion of ACTIONAID's research is that in our evalua-tions and other research there is a need to evaluate the 'value added' by partic-ipatory approaches. This can be done by asking simple questions about what an agency 'learned' through the use of participatory approaches and how their actual interventions changed as a result of this learning. If an agency is making extensive use of PRA and the kinds of approach tried out in this study, then it should be able to report the key differences both in the perceptions of different groups of people and between these perceptions and those of the agency itself. Many NGOs (both local and international) are reluctant to admit either that they themselves do carry with them their own agenda about 'what needs to be done' or that the interests of different groups of people are complex and are bound to conflict, to some extent, with this agenda.

A possible alternative to using PRA is to use conventional survey approach-es but to discuss the initial results as widely as possible both with staff and with different community groups. This kind of approach has been used by Proshika in Bangladesh. Another method used by ACTIONAID in Bangladesh in relation to its Savings and Credit Programme has been to set up 'tracer' surveys focus-ing on those people who have had to drop out of the community groups or 'shomitis' through which these programmes all work. This kind of 'beneficiary assessment' is cost effective as it both targets those people who have had to withdraw from a programme and offers an opportunity for them to provide feed-back on how programme design can be improved.

Implications of ACTIONAID's Research for the Evaluation of Social Development

The major contribution of this research has been to show that local communi-ties can and do assess the impact of development interventions, using a wide variety of indicators, and that agencies need to improve their capacities to listen and to interpret what is happening around them. Formal monitoring systems may be needed to generate particular types of information, but there is a danger they may reduce the capacity of front-line staff to listen, interpret, and report on what is happening on the ground – both 'expected' and 'unexpected' outcomes.

An important conclusion is that in the assessment of impact, a wide variety of methods should be employed; and that it may be a mistake to rely too heavily on any one set of methods, however 'participatory'. Both project staff and evaluators need to be more critical about the use of participatory methodologies in general, and PRA in particular, and our research emphasises the need to make better use of existing information sources and of people's time. We have experienced difficulties in trying to aggregate from a wide diversity of perceptions and indicators, and have found that in some situations staff are reluctant to acknowledge the full diversity of peoples' views, especially where these differ from those held by the staff themselves.

Although the research was initially concerned with 'indicators' in a traditional sense, it has shown the value of focusing on changes in the indicators themselves, or 'meta-indicators' as a way of understanding long-term changes in peoples' attitudes and priorities. 'Capturing' these long-term changes requires far better methods than are normally used for recording and monitoring the views and perceptions of key stakeholders throughout the life cycle of a project intervention.

4.3

NGO Performance: What Breeds Success?

Michael Edwards

All NGOs want to make the best use possible of their limited resources in order to achieve the greatest, sustained impact on poverty and powerlessness in a cost-effective manner. But how are these goals to be achieved? This is a question that has puzzled NGOs, official aid agencies and academics for many years. It has proven extremely difficult to answer, and in any case there are no universal answers to it because the appropriate strategies for achieving different forms of impact in different contexts vary greatly. Yet without convincing answers to questions about impact, cost-effectiveness and sustainability it is not possible for NGOs to achieve their mission to serve others in the best way possible.

This section reports on one study which proposed to identify the factors underlying the impact, sustainability and cost-effectiveness of two NGOs in India – the People's Rural Education Movement (PREM) in Orissa and Urmul in Rajasthan – and two projects implemented by Save the Children Fund-UK in Bangladesh. Importantly, the study also aimed to help the staff of these agencies to reflect on their work in a systematic way, leaving behind additional capacity to continue this process in the form of methods, techniques and questions. To do this full use was made of participatory approaches, especially PRA techniques. The use of these techniques is comparatively rare in organisational assessment; this study demonstrates that they can be powerful vehicles to improve both our understanding of development dynamics and the capacity of NGO staff to reflect on their work, especially when combined with secondary research and quantitative analysis.

The main hypothesis of the study was that impact, sustainability and cost-effectiveness are the result of an interaction between external influences (context) and internal influences (organisational choices), at each point in time. This may seem an obvious point, yet it is often neglected in evaluations of NGO work which looks for clues inside the community or in wider economic and political forces, while ignoring the impact of the NGO itself as an organisation – the approaches it uses in its work, the people it employs, how decisions are made, and so on. These organisational factors are crucial in determining development performance. However, interactions between internal and external factors are very complex, and highly dynamic; it is therefore difficult for conventional research, which takes only a snapshot of the current situation, to unravel them. By using techniques such as organisational time-lines it is possible to shed more light on how different influences combine over time. The full results of the study are presented in a Working Paper published by Save the Children Fund (available from Kathmandu, New Delhi, Dhaka or London) entitled 'NGO Performance: What Breeds Success?'.

Methods
Three sets of methods were used in combination with each other throughout the study:

1. A review of existing documents including secondary literature (SCF files, NGO publicity material, etc.), annual reports and accounts, evaluation and research reports, outputs from monitoring systems and staff profile over time.

2. Semi-structured interviews and discussions, with NGO staff at different levels (individually and in groups), with others (e.g. local government, SCF staff) and with members of communities and participants in programmes (men, women, children and people of different castes).

3. PRA techniques during meetings and field visits, including:

- direct observation by mixed research teams;
- critical incident analysis (asking people to recall something that happened to support a point they were making);
- organisational time-lines (to show how an agency or programme had developed since its foundation or the beginning of its work);
- diagrams to show the structure of the organisation, its activities, and its linkages with other groups and organisations;
- time allocation charts (to map the time spent by staff in different tasks);
- flowcharts (to illustrate how one programme or activity is related to another);
- spider diagrams (to evaluate progress towards different objectives);
- balance diagrams (a method developed on the spot to examine what turned out to be a critical balance between different types of activity in the overall programme).

Examples of the outputs of these exercises are given throughout this section. To combat bias a standard framework of questions was used (prepared and distributed beforehand), the same exercises were used with each agency visited, and the results were cross-checked both against other sources of information and against the same diagram drawn by a different level of staff, or a different part of the organisation. Each visit began with a workshop for staff and involved the production of time-lines, and structure/activity diagrams. The next three days were spent in the field (with more PRA exercises, including time-allocation charts); and the final day took the form of another workshop to explore the preliminary results (using spider and balance diagrams). The time-lines, structure and activity diagrams, and spider diagrams were the most successful techniques used. In all cases participants were encouraged to produce their own versions of diagrams rather than follow a set format. The PRA techniques were particularly useful in the study in:

- building capacity for self-reflection; spider diagrams, for example, proved an excellent way of illuminating different views about progress among staff or in communities in a powerful and accessible way;

- providing a focus for group discussion around key points to emerge from the diagrams; organisational time-lines, for example, stimulated an enormous amount of discussion about what had happened when, and why, allowing different interpretations to be created and challenged along the way. By drawing time-lines on large sheets of paper it was possible for people physically to walk around and across them, pausing to identify critical moments in the life of a project and holding small group discussions about why they were important;

- codifying, presenting and analysing large amounts of information; the exercises (and the other methods used) produced hundreds of flip-chart sheets and notebooks full of observations. Without visual ways of summarising this material it would have been impossible to have a sensible discussion about the results. For example, the spider diagrams produced by different groups were overlaid to produce one version which represented the consensus scores along each objective; time allocation charts for large numbers of staff were pooled to reveal the average amount of time spent on each activity; and secondary data on costs and benefits were recalculated from budgets and annual reports, to be presented in a single table.

On the other hand, the 'hard' data from secondary research and budget analysis about numbers of beneficiaries, programme costs and so on proved very influential, especially inside SCF. It was the combination of striking visual results (from the PRA diagrams) with cost–benefit data that was important; one without the other would not have been so powerful. Bureaucracies need numbers as well as pictures if they are to take notice! This was despite the fact that the results (especially the averages and cost–benefit calculations) were highly imperfect. But the trade-off between rigour and accessibility was, in my view, a reasonable one. The study did produce a set of empirically based conclusions which are reasonably reliable and representative, while simultaneously providing a vehicle for critical reflection and analysis among staff and communities. This resulted in both increased capacity for organisational self-assessment in the future (feeding through, one hopes, into more benefits for poor people in the long run), and valuable insights into NGO performance which should make a useful contribution to the wider literature. This is not to say that the balance between the two objectives was right – it was not. There was not enough emphasis on training and capacity enhancement (something which is being corrected in the next round); the interpretation of results (the key area) was too dependent on myself, and therefore very much represents my own views of what the results tell us; follow-up was disappointing (though feedback from the eventual report was positive in most cases, and other NGOs in India have now expressed a wish to take part in a second round of similar exercises); and the field visits were inadequately prepared. This led to suspicions among some of the organisations as to the motives of the exercise ('just another academic from outside who's come to take our knowledge', as one put it to me). It took a full day of discussion to air these feelings and find a consensus on which to move forward.

The approach used in this exercise did not resolve the dilemma faced by all external agencies who use participatory techniques in their work – the 'extraction' of information for agency use went hand in hand with the 'empowerment' of staff and others through the process of capacity enhancement. Indeed, these dual goals were always, and transparently, a part of the exercise. Personally, I doubt that this dilemma can ever be fully resolved; but it can and should be managed more effectively. We tried to achieve this by being honest about the motives of the exercise from the word go; by only working with organisations who actively requested that they be included; by pre-circulating a framework of questions and encouraging each organisation to discuss them independently of the research team, being honest about which they thought were relevant, which could be dropped, and what others might be included; by being as open and flexible as possible in terms of timing, techniques and reporting back; and by stipulating that nothing would be published without the explicit consent of all the agencies involved.

As the results emerged (especially in the preliminary written report) it also became clear that there would be substantive disagreement in some areas. This affected the SCF programmes in Bangladesh in particular, with some staff feeling that I had underestimated the importance of decisions taken by SCF Headquarters in London, and apportioned too much responsibility for disappointing results to factors internal to the organisation in the field. It took another four months or so to negotiate a form of words in the final report to satisfy these concerns, while remaining true to the actual findings of the field-work. The use of PRA techniques in organisational settings should only be contemplated by organisations which are prepared to reflect on their performance seriously and openly, and to change themselves as a result. For NGOs (or other agencies) which are committed to putting their participatory principles into practice, such methods can be invaluable in identifying ways forward, especially when used in conjunction with other methods which give the results more credibility in bureaucratic settings.

Findings

The underlying bench-mark against which NGO performance was measured was the ability to facilitate sustained improvements in capacities and livelihoods among poor people. None of the four agencies aims to provide services to poor people indefinitely: instead they aim to promote community management of services, confidence and organisational capacity at grass-roots level, sustainable improvements in the ownership and management of assets and links to government and other permanent structures. NGOs which aim to deliver services themselves over the long term face a different set of performance criteria. The conclusions of this study do not apply to them.

Measured against this bench-mark, the four agencies had widely varying patterns of impact, sustainability and cost-effectiveness. They ranged from very high impact on both material and social/organisational indicators across a population of over 800,000 to low impact on these two dimensions among a population of under 40,000. The estimated ratio of total costs per beneficiary ranged from £0.17 to £4.53. In explaining these variations the following overall conclusions emerged.

External Influences

Conclusion One: context is crucial but not determinant; therefore, organisational choices always provide some room for manoeuvre.

The influence of external factors comes through loud and clear. Rural Bangladesh offers a much less attractive environment for grass-roots level organisation than Orissa (India). It simply would not be possible to transfer many of the successful strategies used by one agency to another context. The major influences in the external environment seem to be social and political rather than economic: high levels of poverty and wide gaps in the satisfaction of basic needs and the provision of health and education services exist in all four areas, yet the relative success of each organisation in tackling these problems varies greatly. The social homogeneity of the communities in which the NGO works is an important factor in explaining these variations, as is the attitude of local government to NGO work and the amount of political space made available by the state and local elites for grass-roots mobilisation. PREM in Orissa has been able to promote the development of a statewide federation of autonomous grass-roots organisations which are capable of making claims and running programmes themselves; hence, the impact of PREM's work, multiplied through the federation, is much greater than that of the other agencies. But PREM enjoyed a favourable context for this strategy: homogeneous communities (of tribal people and fisherfolk) which organised themselves fairly easily, and a tolerant political environment which enabled the federation to grow stronger. Neither of these conditions applies in rural Bangladesh, or in Rajasthan where Urmul works.

Internal Influences

Conclusion Two: be clear about where you are heading in the long term, and do not be distracted (unless there is a very good reason to change along the way).

Organisations which have a clear and shared vision of what they want to achieve, and stick to it over time, tend to obtain better results than agencies which change their goals too often, or spread themselves too thinly. Inspirational but not overbearing leadership is crucial here, as is a shared analysis of development, and a strong set of guiding values and principles. If the aim is 'empowerment', there must be a genuine commitment to hand over power and responsibility and to de-emphasise the intermediary (NGO).

Although this can be taken to extremes (as when an organisation refuses to adapt its goals to a changing context), the absence of a clear long-term vision tends to make it more difficult to link goals with strategies and to know when to say 'no' to new activities. There will always be a temptation to accept new funding or responsibilities (for example, a new government education scheme or an offer from an external donor to provide resources in return for children to be sponsored), and where health and other needs are great (and funding pressures are acute) the pressure to accept will be considerable. However, such activities can prove a diversion from the core, ongoing work of the organisation and result in too little time being spent on capacity enhancement, institutional development, and asset building. This is a particular problem where an NGO works as a contractor to government, since the amount of independence and flexibility it retains will be limited and internal direction and momentum may be lost. In the case of Urmul in Rajasthan, for example, every effort was made to minimise the knock-on effects of operating the ICDS (child health, nutrition

109

and education) programme on behalf of the state government, but this absorbed a huge amount of time and energy from key staff and left some of the village level groups under-supported, especially as Urmul was under constant pressure to scale-up the ICDS programme without much increase in capacity.

Or take the example of SCF in Bangladesh. Every time there was a change of Field Director in Dhaka there was also a change of programme focus on the ground: from relief to health, to education and most recently to credit provision. In combination with other organisational problems, this detracted from the continuity and depth of involvement at grass-roots level which are required to address complex structural problems of power and resources.

Conclusion Three: get the balance right between different strategies right from the beginning, especially between material and social/organisational development, and keep it there over time.

Some combinations of strategy seem to work against impact and effectiveness, as when an organisation takes on too many different roles at once. Others, however, have the opposite effect, and reinforce each other so that 'the whole becomes more than the sum of its parts'. This seems particularly true of the combination between material improvements in people's lives (assets, incomes and services), and improvements in their confidence, awareness and organisational capacities. It is this balance which holds the key to results. When the balance moves too far towards the material dimension, any impact may be unsustainable or fail to reach the very poor. Organisational sustainability is a more difficult goal to reach than financial sustainability. On the other hand, if the balance moves too far towards the social or organisational, people may become bored with a process that fails to provide material improvements in their lives. The best results are achieved where there is a more-or-less equal balance between the two from the start of the programme, all the time. This is obviously difficult to do in some situations, and organisations which use relief or service provision as an 'entry point' must be particularly careful that the balance is created or restored as soon as is practicable. If there has to be a 'trade-off' between the two, it may be better to de-emphasise the material dimension for a while so that social and organisational goals can be secured. Equally, this balance and the way in which it changes over time has to be conditioned by the needs, perceptions and priorities of the people with whom the NGO is working. Otherwise programmes may not be relevant to real needs and preferences, and any impact may be short-lived.

The best example of this from the study is PREM in Orissa. Here, enormous effort went into awareness-raising, legal education and social organisation among grass-roots organisations right from the start of the programme, but there were material improvements too in the shape of food security (seed and grain banks), land redistribution, health and education services, and credit-and-savings schemes. The benefits from these programmes encouraged people to persevere with their organisational work, while the rise of the federation of grass-roots organisations made it possible for more people to participate in material improvements, and to sustain these programmes over time.

Conclusion Four: always pay attention to 'the basics'.

In NGOs which aim to promote sustained improvements in capacities and livelihoods, certain things (or 'basics') must be attended to: investment in the right people, good communications, continuous learning, closeness to the grass-roots, strong local institutions, an inspirational but not overbearing leadership and participatory planning and management. These are all essential in any context. Yet there is often a tendency among NGOs to neglect them, and this always has adverse consequences. When results have been disappointing in the four cases studied here, one of the main reasons has usually been the neglect of one or more of these 'basics'. This is particularly so with organisations which take on too much or lose their sense of direction: 'the basics' are squeezed out or relegated or even forgotten completely. By contrast, building confidence and capacity at the grass-roots can bring remarkable results: in Orissa the rate of graduation of autonomous grass-roots organisations is the key to a strategy which has achieved a very large impact at a very low cost. Results have been scaled-up while keeping quality high and core costs low. Interestingly, formal systems for strategic planning, monitoring and evaluation seem to be less important than informal ones in keeping an organisation effective, so long as these informal systems are enforced. However, in large organisations or agencies which concentrate on advocacy, more formal systems may be required.

The outputs of the PRA exercises were particularly useful in helping staff of the four organisations to examine these issues. For example, simple structure provided an excellent foundation for discussing the relative merits of hierarchical versus horizontal linkages. Time allocation diagrams quickly revealed to staff in Urmul (Rajasthan) that they were spending much more time than they had realised in doing things for village income-generation groups (especially production and marketing), than in developing the capacity of groups to do these things for themselves. And 'spider diagrams' provided a graphic illustration of the areas in which different groups within the NGO were more, or less, happy with their progress. The cumulative effect of the PRA exercises and other research was to reveal when and where these 'basics' were being neglected, and what implications this might have for organisational performance. The stage was then set for a further discussion of what to do about it.

Conclusion Five: build as many strong linkages as possible both vertically and horizontally, and use them creatively.

There are many different forms of linkage, and linkages are important for many different reasons: learning, influencing, resource mobilisation and communication. Strong linkages which are properly used are one of the keys to both scaling-up and sustainability. Organisations with weak links tend to have only a localised, short-term impact. Which linkages are most important will vary according to the objectives of the programme, but in programmes which aim to promote sustainable improvements in capacities and livelihoods the links between grass-roots organisations (and their representative structures) and government do most to determine success or failure. Building such representative structures above the village level, and linking them to different parts and levels of government, is critical for sustainable development.

This was a particular problem with the two SCF programmes in Bangladesh, which (until recently when there was a major change of direction in the SCF programme) have tended to isolate themselves from other NGOs and the lessons they could have taught. For example, the credit programme established in the River Project in 1989 did not build on established practice elsewhere in Bangladesh, resulting in costs which where many times higher per group, and were simply unsustainable. In contrast, the grass-roots organisations supported by PREM in Orissa have deliberately linked into the political and administrative structure at all levels (with 360 of their representatives elected to various offices), so that they have been able to influence the distribution of state resources and other policies to the benefit of marginalised groups.

The Role of Donors
Conclusion Six: make sure you adjust your policies and procedures so that they support the things that lead to success, and do not exacerbate the problems.

Although SCF does not emerge as the most influential factor in any of the case studies, it is clear that what SCF and other donors do or do not do can make success easier or more difficult to achieve. In this respect, the situation in Bangladesh is very different to that in India, since both case studies in Bangladesh were implemented directly by SCF. The results of this approach are not encouraging, though this does not mean that it is impossible for such operational programmes to be successful. In India, the issue is whether the way in which SCF has operated added to or detracted from the success of local partners. There is little evidence to suggest that it has done either in any significant sense, but there is clearly more potential for SCF to 'add more value' through its partnerships by enabling Indian NGOs to have more access to the 'non-funding support' that they want: international linkages, learning from experience, exchanges and inputs on specific issues and a critical dialogue. For SCF the message is clear: develop the same characteristics at all levels of SCF that, as this study shows, underpin successful local NGO performance – investment in the basics, a clear vision and the determination to stick to it, strong linkages, and a real willingness to pull back from an operational role so that others can develop and utilise their own capacities to the full.

Conclusions

In a report of this brevity, and a study of this complexity, it is only possible to sketch an outline of the factors that determine NGO performance. In all cases, impact, sustainability and cost-effectiveness are determined by combinations of internal and external factors which are unique to each NGO at each point in time. Yet there is sufficient commonality in the findings to suggest that there are patterns at work, and that NGO performance is not simply a 'lottery' dependent on the external environment in which an organisation finds itself working. In other words, conscious action can be taken to improve performance even when context is difficult (as it nearly always is). In particular, sustainable impact will never be achieved without:

• assets, confidence, skills, capacities and institutions at the grass-roots level;
• mechanisms to link people and institutions with actors and decisions higher up the system.

The evidence of this study shows that NGOs which succeed in tackling both areas obtain the best results. Furthermore, there are two prime factors underlying the relative success or failure of intermediary NGOs in this process: one is the quality of the presence of the NGO over the long term, and the other is continuous learning. Participatory techniques have considerable – and thus far unrealised – potential in unlocking these complex patterns of cause and effect while simultaneously enhancing NGO capacity for self-assessment and critical reflection.

More generally, the study leads to a number of general conclusions about assessing the impact of NGO programmes. It is certainly possible to evaluate the impact of NGO activities from a social as well as an economic perspective in ways which achieve a reasonable level of rigour, participation and trade-offs in terms of time and resources. We can do better in evaluation without large-scale resources or radical conceptual shifts. There is a great deal of potential in the use of participatory methods in impact evaluation (PRA), especially when combined with other approaches such as solid secondary research and detailed financial analysis. Whatever methods are used they must cover all the organisations and linkages that are relevant (donors, local government, 'partners').

Finally, because this form of evaluation reveals uncomfortable issues for donors as well as 'recipients', it should not be undertaken by agencies which lack openness and commitment to change. Social development evaluation requires evaluators and institutions that are socially developed (creative, participatory, etc.)! Removing barriers to these attitudes and building capacities is just as important in improving impact evaluation as the development of better techniques.

4.4

The Evaluation of an Ongoing Educational Programme

Maria Christina Garcia

Introduction

This evaluation is concerned with two common problems faced by the external evaluator of social and educational programmes. The first is that many ongoing programmes do not have baseline data or continual follow-up procedures, thus forcing the evaluator to develop innovative and creative methods to overcome this obstacle. The second difficulty comes from the multi-dimensional nature of many such programmes, making it necessary for a multifaceted evaluation that uses multiple approaches and methods.

The Programme

A brief outline of the programme is necessary in order to understand the evaluation undertaken. Cuclí Cuclí (name of a children's game) is a national educational programme designed to promote interest and knowledge in science, scientific thinking and desire for knowledge in Colombia's primary schoolchildren. It also has a political side, as it aims to develop healthy attitudes in young children concerning solidarity, respect for differences, responsibility and autonomy. It uses two basic materials – children's magazines and posters – which are delivered to the individual schools. These materials each deal with a specific theme using a variety of approaches. These themes include energy, time, water, and approaches include scientific knowledge, stories, poetry, games, experiments etc.

The programme operates through the National Institute for the Promotion of Science and Research (Colciencias). Human resources include a team of Colciencias experts, consultants and individuals from the National University of Colombia. It is sent by mail to all the state schools both in rural and urban areas, which number around 35,000, and depending on the size of the school between two and five examples of each material are sent to each.

Why the Evaluation?

One of the issues that must be considered in any external evaluation is the motive for carrying out an evaluation, as well as the commitment of programme actors to cooperate with and support the work. The reason being that if the beneficiaries do not see the need for the evaluation, the task of the evaluator will be difficult and in some cases impossible. Furthermore, it needs to be decided who will use and benefit from the information gained from the evaluation. In the Cuclí Cuclí experience, an evaluation which did not help to improve either programme development or implementation seemed to us to be neither worthwhile nor ethical.

From the social point of view there were several reasons why the evaluation was worthwhile. Cuclí Cuclí represents a considerable national investment in a country where there is an agreed need for support for education but resources are scarce. The programme has special importance given its coverage of all state schools, its international recognition and the great potential to be disseminated or replicated in other places. This makes an evaluation very necessary but adds to its complexity. A further reason was that Colciencias wanted to confirm that the programme had been as expected before analysing and introducing possible new programme components. The team of authors and designers of the programme were also interested in the evaluation of the use and acceptance of the programme and the extent to which the teachers incorporate it into their lessons. Finally, it was also necessary to present a report to the financing organisation, the World Bank.

CINDE's Perspective

CINDE agreed with the programme's aim with respect to the social context and considered that the scarce resources available for education should be invested in the most profitable way. CINDE was asked by Colciencias and the programme's designers to carry out the evaluation as an external exercise. For CINDE it was important that if any needs of either the programme or the beneficieries were identified during the evaluation they would be responded to in any new programme components.

Problems to be Faced

The evaluation faced several difficulties which might be common to the other experiences, and which are therefore worthy of being shared with a wider audience.

- The programme had been operating for six years with neither continuous monitoring nor designed evaluation mechanisms. The project team was the conceiver and initiator of the programme and felt a high degree of protectiveness towards it.

- The normal and frequent tensions between the project team, the host and support organisation and the financial agency did exist and needed to be dealt with.
- The evaluation was conceived of as an external exercise which is not always

the best or most participatory approach and only a specific, brief time period was set aside for it.

• The target groups had not been involved in the design or testing of the programme or materials.

Given the above reasons, special attention was paid to involving the team in the design of the evaluation and the definition of the criteria of what to evaluate as well as how to do it. Time and energy were invested in this so that the final result would be comprehensive, objective and participatory.

The Evaluation Design and Process
What should be Evaluated?
After a number of meetings and interviews with the project coordinator, the directors of Colciencias and the programme authors the main issues were agreed upon. The following aspects were included in the evaluation plan:

1. Coverage in relation to the expectation of a nationwide scale.

2. Quality of the programme material, regarding its suitability for the children's characteristics and origins and as a means of instruction.

3. Implementation – the use of the material in the schools.

4. Impact of the programme on the children, teachers, schools and others.

How should the Evaluation be Carried Out?
This refers to the issue of methodology given the variety of information to be evaluated and the need of an integral programme analysis. Different information should be gathered in different ways, and in the following order:

• documentation of the project history, design and implementation and stakeholders;
• surveys with different stakeholders;
• personal interviews;
• field visits and direct observation;
• tests for the children – knowledge, cognitive development and attitude tests.

Who should be Involved?
Different stakeholders were involved to provide different perspectives about the programme, including those who support and direct the project at an institu-

tional level as well as the team of project authors and designers. Also included were the people involved in the distribution of the materials – the local and, most important of all, regional authorities – and the consumers of the programme – the children and teachers.

Also there was a group of experts on education, child development, children's text and child communication who were specially selected to evaluate the quality of the materials from a different perspective. A guide was developed for them to follow.

The Purpose of the Evaluation
The main purpose of the evaluation was twofold:

- To provide feedback regarding the programme and recommendations for its improvement, directed first to the team then to the supporter of the institution and through them the financing agency.

- To develop instruments for future monitoring and process evaluation of the programme.

The Process
The evaluation process involved different aspects and methodological approaches due to the variety of information and analysis required. In this way the evaluation became multifaceted and pluralistic in its approach, in order to give full and adequate answers to questions concerning the programme's quality, relevancy and implementation.

The aspects to be evaluated, the information required and the approach or means necessary are in the following chart.

The Sample
The samples were designed to overcome the obstacle of a lack of initial baseline information on the programme and the children. A system was to designed which would produce samples (of schools) with different levels of exposure to the programme: continuous and total; discontinuous and scarce numbers; not received at all. Also different levels of implementation of the programme schools were considered or used: low rate of practice without external support and Cuclí-schools (Cuclí-escuelas), in which an added experimental programme of teacher motivation and training was carried out. The sample group replaced the baseline information for comparison purposes, and so permitted an evaluation of programme impact.

118

Table 4.1 The Process of the Evaluation

Object	Aspect	Means	Approach
I. Quality of the material	Relevancy to the children's characteristic: Origin: rural/urban poor communities, different ethnic groups	Group of experts on education, communi-cation, language, science Analysis of materials, an evaluation guide	Mainly quantitative
	Ages 7–12 Levels of literacy Children's interests Knowledge and capabilities of the children Adequate language and style used. Communication established with the child Scientific content Relation with the curriculum and real possibilities of schools.	Individual reports Joint workshop with the group of experts and the research team final report and recommendations Workshop and exchange between the exchange authors and the team Final Report and recommendations	Team participation
II. Coverage	Is the programme intended for all or the majority of (state) schools? Does the programme arrive at those schools? When the programme is received is it made accessible to pupils and teachers?	Survey (Samples) Surveys and interviews (visits)	Quantitative Quantitative – Qualitative
III. Use	Do teachers know the programme and materials? Do the children know the programme and materials? Where are they kept in the schools? Who uses them? How are they used? Children's knowledge of the programme Comprehension of themes by the children	Surveys Interviews with teachers and headmasters Surveys Interviews with Visits, observation and interviews	Qualitative and quantitative Qualitative and quantitative Qualitative

119

Object	Aspect	Means	Approach
IV. Impact on children	Are the children attracted to the material?	Visits:	Quantitative
	Children's interest in science Curiosity and interest in knowledge Attitudes toward gender, religion, tolerance, solidarity, and respect Cognitive development	Tests and questionaires: Pilot experience	
V. Impact on the schools/ teacher	Do the teachers know the objectives of the programme?	Survey	Qualitative and quantitative
	Do they use it? Why do they? Why don't they? How do they use it? Do they find the programme useful or not? What are the suggestions, worries and wishes connected to the programme? Have any other activities been born from working with the programme?	Interviews, visits	Quantitative

Three samples were designed. The first was a national sample of 1,000 schools from all departments (states), including proportionally both rural and urban schools. It was designed to replicate the real distribution of schools and children in Colombia and also within the individual department according to the size of the cities and towns. Together with sample 2, sample 1 was used to test the programme coverage, reception and usage of material on a national level.

The second sample also consisted of 1,000 schools, bringing the total sample up to 2,000. It was used with sample 1 to test the national coverage aspect plus a third sample of 300 schools which were to be visited and which represented the range of different exposures to the programme. These schools were chosen on a regional basis using a standardised system of the Colombian National Institute for the Promotion of Sciences (Colciencias) in order to ensure compatible data. The other factor in the selection was the distance between the

schools in an effort to make the field visit and work feasible.
The 300 schools for the third sample were selected to present the following criteria:

- no use with non-arrival or very low arrival;
- low use with normal arrival;
- high use with normal arrival;
- high use, motivation and training for teachers (Cuclí-escuelas).

Each of these 300 schools were visited and interviews were carried out with teachers, headteachers, education authorities and children. Six thousand children were examined on knowledge and attitude using tests specifically designed and tested for the programme. From the second sample 2,000 teachers were surveyed, and from the third 600 were interviewed.

An additional pilot experience was set up using 20% of sample 3 schools. This tested the materials and applied a cognitive development test to evaluate the impact of the programme on areas of child development.

Although it is not the purpose of this study to discuss the results of the evaluation, but rather its process and the lessons learned from the experiences, there follows a brief synthesis of the main conclusions.

The Cuclí Cuclí programme was judged very positively as regards its conception, intention, contents and aims. The team which created the materials was highly praised by the experts for their dedication, commitment, creative ability and openness to change, qualities reflected in the materials they produced: concepts, contents, methods of explanation and use of image. However, a number of recommendations were made to take more account of the heteregenous characteristics of the children.

Cuclí Cuclí has been successfully received into educational institutions which is an important factor. This indicates the efficiency of the distribution system. It is still not possible to speak of a uniform use, and even less of a desired level of understanding and integration of the programme in the schools. The clue to the differences seems to be the involvement of the teachers in the programme. The main recommendation was the introduction of training for teachers.

Lessons

The main lessons learned regarding the evaluation of social or educational development programmes are as follows:

- Evaluation requires quantitative and qualitative information. Many times qualitative information can be the means to interpret and highlight quantitative information about the impact.

- It is necessary to involve stakeholders operating at different levels. Promoting frequent dialogue between stakeholders increases the chance that the programme's quality will be improved as well as highlights its impact.

- Evaluation should be a learning exercise which enables stakeholders to improve their own practice. It should not remain a purely academic exercise.

- The process should be seen in as broad a light as possible, using creative methods when initial or process information does not exist. For evaluations of ongoing processes that have not included monitoring and baseline data, a wider range of information should be used to evaluate the impact.

- Participation in the evaluation process is not only a right of those involved in the programme, but also the only way to promote its use and so maintain the result.

- External evaluation is not the best alternative for ongoing processes and should be done with the approval and participation of other stakeholders.

- When an external evaluation is the only option available, it should be orientated towards developing data to provide a baseline and instruments for monitoring a future continuous evaluation.

4.5

Institutional Learning in a Process-Oriented Programme: Monitoring and Evaluation of the Community Empowerment Programme in South Wollo, Ethiopia

Terry Bergdall

The 'Community Empowerment Programme' (CEP) is a pilot project funded by the Swedish International Development Cooperation Agency (SIDA) as an integral part of preparations for a major long-term support programme to the Amhara Region in northeast Ethiopia. It has operated in five western *woredas* (districts), of the South Wollo Zone since April 1994.

As a pilot project, CEP is an experimental activity for discerning effective approaches for catalysing local initiatives and community responsibility for development in rural areas. CEP was not designed or launched as a total package with a detailed 'blueprint.' In contrast, it emerged after a series of activities and continues to evolve as a 'process-oriented' programme. It began by holding a series of 'Community Participation Workshops' (CPW) within *kires*, the small traditional self-help organisations found across Ethiopia that provide assistance to community members during important social events like funerals and weddings.

From the beginning, monitoring and evaluation have been seen as crucial elements in the enterprise. As consultants engaged by SIDA to support the programme, we have attempted to address several key questions as we have guided monitoring and evaluation work within the project. It has been our assumption that an effective monitoring and evaluation system must be (a) quantitative, (b) qualitative and (c) enable institutional learning to take place. The monitoring and evaluation work of the past two years, therefore, has addressed these three primary concerns. First, it has focused on quantitative issues: 'what has happened in programme areas after implementation began, when did it happen, where did it happen, how much of it happened?' Second, it has focused on qualitative issues: 'what important changes have occurred and how are these changes perceived?' Third, and perhaps most important, it has focused on issues related to organisational learning: 'what new collective understandings have emerged about participation, community empowerment and bottom-up development through programme activities?'

The Internal Monitoring System

The CEP internal monitoring system was created in April 1995 and comprised collecting quantitative and qualitative information. In addition, the monitoring and evaluation system included background information and writing 'documentation reports' of particular activities taking place within every community involved in the programme. An aspiration of the monitoring and evaluation design was to engage all of the programme's stakeholders in a process of institutional learning. The stakeholders included the *kires* (communities); various levels of government; SIDA and the consulting consortium overseeing the planning process for the future long-term programme.

All learning involves the receiving, sorting, and retaining of information. For individuals and groups alike, 'knowledge' is the result of a complex process of managing vast amounts of information. Behaviour, the way people act and do things, is very closely linked to their understanding and perception of the world in which they live. Change in perceptions, i.e., 'knowledge', is a prerequisite to lasting change in behaviour. By extension, social change involves a collective consensus about agreed upon perceptions and their importance. The monitoring and evaluation system within CEP was, therefore, conceived of as more than a mere tool for obtaining information about the progress of a particular programme; it was envisioned as an important mechanism for fostering change. At its broadest, this is the implied meaning of 'institutional learning' within a social development programme.

Quantitative Monitoring

Numbers are fascinating. There is the perception among many people in the development community that monitoring and evaluation is simply not serious if it does not provide a lot of numbers to be examined and analysed. Even though the consultancy team of which I was a part was rather sceptical about the significance of collecting a lot of numbers, we wanted to give appropriate attention to the gathering and analysis of quantitative monitoring information. As will be seen, the more we worked with assisting the project to create its design for quantitative monitoring, the more we became enamoured with its illusive potential.

As the monitoring effort began with CEP, a number of challenges in creating a quantitative system were identified. These included the need to determine key indicators relevant to the objective of the programme, to create a manageable system which was focused and limited in the amount of information collected, and to devise a simple and effective system for collecting, storing and retrieving information. The initial design of the quantitative system was, however, overly ambitious in its attempt to gather data in relation to a series of questions:

- What has been done in the community?
- How much has been done by the community?
- Who did the work?
- What kind of local maintenance has been done following the development activities?
- How much local investment is being made?
- What are the facilitation capabilities and commitment of *kire* coordinators?

The initial design called for the tracking of 27 typical development activities (e.g., terracing, spring protection, planting seedlings, etc.) which emerged from the action plans produced by *kire* members at the earliest CPWs. Perhaps most ambitious of all, the design called for comprehensive collection of information about all activities undertaken with the community and then distinguishing between activities accomplished on the basis of 'local initiative' and those through 'mobilisation'.

Local initiative referred to development undertakings that were planned and implemented by small groups of people. This did not eliminate the possibility of some external advice or assistance, but such help was to come in response to the local initiatives: community people remained the primary actors and were essentially responsible for organising and implementing work on their own. Fundamental 'ownership' of the project was theirs. Local initiatives could be undertaken by the *kire* organisation itself or by smaller groups or individuals within the *kires*.

Mobilisation referred to development undertakings that were essentially conceived of, planned, and organised by external agencies, be they government bodies, governmental 'development agents' or non-government organisations, even though such undertakings might be accomplished with the 'participation' of community labour. Realisation of development 'quotas' or 'targets' planned by officials outside the immediate community (i.e., the *kire*) were considered examples of mobilisation. 'Food for Work' was considered a mobilisation activity too, because, if not actually planned by external officials, the primary stimulus for the activity was food payments originating from outside of the community.

The intention of this data collection was to provide a large range of options for data analysis and comparison. Some of the anticipated possibilities were:

- absolute and relative frequency of 27 development activities which could be further broken down into frequencies of mobilisation and frequencies of local initiative;
- the types of development activities most typically planned by women, men and youth;

- comparisons of types of development activity for mobilisation and local initiative both before and after the CPW;
- the total amount of work done through mobilisation and local initiative in each of the 27 development activities, with comparisons of totals both before and after the CPW;
- the type of maintenance of each development activity for mobilisation and local initiative, both before and after the CPW;
- both material and cash investment by the *kires* in development activities for mobilisation and local initiative before and after the CPW (after the CPW, this could be analysed relative to each of the three follow-up visits);
- the number of *kire* coordinators trained in facilitation skills by the categories of women, men and youth;
- *kire* coordinators' actual participation as facilitators in the workshops during follow-up visit number three in each kire;
- assessments of each *kire*'s capability of continuing the CEP process on their own once visits by the facilitators have been completed;
- the analysis of all this information in the aggregate or disaggregate by *woredas* and other geographical divisions.

In June and July 1995, the computerised database for the quantitative monitoring system was created and tested; the cumulative data to that point was entered, questions were raised about the data and the means of verification. This revealed several serious questions about the ambitions and design of the quantitative monitoring system. These were thoroughly discussed by the Lead Facilitators and MAP consultants resulting in several conclusions about the data to be monitored.

- It was initially thought to be important to be able to make two comparisons: one between what had happened relative to local initiative work for the two years prior to a *kire*'s Community Participation Workshop (CPW) and what happened in the two years afterwards; a second between accomplishments through mobilisation efforts and those through local initiative efforts. However, data for both comparisons proved to be problematic. *Kire* members could not be precise relative to any of the information categories, nor was there any way for the facilitators to verify the data.

- Another category of data originally envisioned was the tracking of material and cash investments made by the *kires* to see if there was any substantive change over time. This also proved problematic, with estimates by *kire* members clearly imprecise and varying greatly from *kire* to *kire* and from *woreda* to *woreda*. Again, there was no one to accurately quantify or verify the data being reported.

• Finally, all data collected had focused exclusively on action plans created by the *kires*; nothing was systematically being collected about priority development needs. There was also a lack of clarity on the key question in this regard – should the listed needs be only those that the *kire* thought it could deal with through its own resources and know-how, or should the development needs be irrespective of the *kire*'s ability to resolve them?

Consequently, major revisions to the quantitative monitoring system were made in March 1996. The decisions made and the actions taken for collecting data were the following:

• Given the problems of collecting and verifying accurate data, all information relative to past accomplishments, be they through local initiative or mobilisation, were eliminated. Eliminated, too, was any attempt to quantify material and cash investments made by the *kires* in their development activities. All data collection on mobilisation work was also eliminated; only data pertaining to local initiatives were retained.

• It was decided that information would be collected on development needs by recording priority needs identified in CPWs irrespective of a *kire*'s ability to resolve them. Though this data began to be collected, it was not entered and tracked in the computerised database due to the complexity of entering and tracking such diverse data. Compiling and reporting information on the priority development needs was done manually as required.

These revisions resulted in the collection of quantitative information that could be more accurately and verifiably collected and reported on. The information remained, however, quite extensive. The primary improvement was thought to be in the reliability of the data – it did not require 'guesstimates' by *kire* members, and it was verifiable. Data on action plans was simply a matter of reporting, and data on accomplishments could be physically inspected and measured.

In summary, all of these revisions basically amounted to tracking community initiatives occurring after CEP interventions. In addition to tracking the attendance at these events, information is also compiled about 'action plans created during CPWs and follow-up meetings' and 'local initiatives accomplished beyond specific projects planned at the CPWs or follow-up'.

The question still remains, however: what do all of the numbers really mean? The quantitative data thus far compiled raised many interesting questions which need to be illuminated before one can fully understand the significance of the numbers. Below are some of the key issues in interpreting the data:

• Though the distinction between 'local initiative' and 'mobilisation' is stressed in the collection guidelines of the internal monitoring and evaluation system, there is uncertainty as to whether or not the reported numbers really reflect this distinction.

• Not only are there big difficulties in identifying and quantifying 'local initiatives', there is an even a bigger problem in, if not the impossibility of, isolating the crucial stimulus behind such initiatives: though the CEP monitoring and evaluation system is careful not to claim 'credit' for these activities, any serious interpretation of the data needs some assessment of other possible stimuli besides CEP which might account for these local initiatives.

• Attempts at establishing some type of 'control sample' for gaining a better understanding about the quantitative information of communities after CPW and follow-ups reveals something different from what might be expected in any event, even if no CPW had been held.

A follow-up qualitative study is now being planned in a random sample of *kires* where CPWs and follow-ups have taken place to help resolve these issues and to add to a more knowledgeable interpretation of the quantitative information. The major objective of the proposed study will be to add qualitative information to the CEP internal monitoring system so that the numbers reported in the quantitative data can be better understood. Specific sub-objectives of the study will be to investigate and report upon:

• the communities' understanding of 'local initiatives' as reported in the monitoring data;
• an assessment of the reliability of these reported numbers and a qualitative indication of the 'margin of error';
• possible stimuli besides CEP which might account for reported initiatives and a discussion of their importance;
• some comparative indication of the significance of 'local initiatives' reported after CPWs and follow-ups with those in a small sample of *kires* where CPWs have not taken place.

To enhance the direct learning opportunity of the field-work, this follow-up study will be undertaken by a special team of appointed regional officials (most likely from the Bureau of Agriculture and the Office of Women's Affairs). The team will conduct its field-work in six different randomly selected *kires* where CEP has taken place and three nearby 'control' *kires* where it has not. A minimum of three days will be allotted to the team in each of the selected *kires*. Information will be gathered by group discussions, in-depth interviews and personal observations. It is anticipated that findings of this study should provide valuable indicative information for interpreting the extensive quantitative information collected by the programme. The involvement of the regional officials should also greatly add to the participatory nature of the monitoring and evaluation work.

Qualitative Monitoring of CEP
Quantitative information is essential in the monitoring of any development programme, but as the above section illustrates, it has obvious limitations. While such data can more or less provide an indication about 'how much and how many' it is difficult for naked numbers to answer 'so what'. Quantitative information tends to abstract human experience and strip it of its context. Qualitative information serves as a complement to the numerical tracking of local development initiatives by bringing development work 'to life' through stories and anecdotes. These in turn are crucial clues to understanding the dynamics of empowerment. Creating an effective qualitative monitoring system, however, raises a number of questions.

First, how can the monitoring system be participatory? The focus of monitoring activities, even when done in a qualitative way, are often defined by people very distant from the activities which are being monitored. Indicators are identified by specialists, consultants or senior staff who collect information and analyse the results. Programme participants and field staff, if involved at all, are typically asked to review the conclusions of these specialists and offer comments at the end of the process. Participatory monitoring, if it is to be genuine, needs to find practical means for participants and staff to be 'part and parcel' of the entire system on a continuing basis, from beginning to end.

Secondly, how can stakeholders at all levels of the programme be involved in the monitoring process? This is an expansive dimension of the participation question above. The stakeholders of most programmes are many and varied. Creative ways for involving them in practical aspects of the monitoring system need to be found.

Thirdly, how can the information from the monitoring system become a basis of 'organisational learning'. Information is only mildly interesting if it is not put to practical use. There need to be mechanisms for learning from experience and modifying the programme accordingly. Rather than such modifications coming merely from conclusions drawn by senior staff, personnel and stakeholders throughout the entire organisation need a practical way to be involved with the changes. This implies a process for reaching a general consensus about the strengths and weaknesses of programme performance, directions it needs to go in the future, and practical steps to be taken to reach the desired end result.

The design of the monitoring and evaluation system took these questions into serious consideration. The primary approach for qualitative monitoring focused on recording and tracking perceptions of change (this approach built upon the research work of Rick Davis, CDS, Swansea). Change, for several reasons, was thought to be an appropriate subject for qualitative monitoring. With a broad aim to improve the quality of life, monitoring of change can help keep the 'bigger' picture in view. The content of reported change, however, remains specific, tied directly to particular communities.

Change is also a relatively simple concept for people to consider. It requires few predetermined factors. Questions about changes often lead to a host of unanticipated topics, thereby easily enabling people with diverse backgrounds and perspectives to say what is of importance to them. Impressions come easily when comparing conditions 'before' and 'after' and, because it is so uncomplicated, many people can be involved. Yet asking simple questions about the reasons for change is a quick springboard into deeper thinking about more complex issues.

The model adopted by CEP attempted to involve people at all levels of the programme directly in the monitoring process. It included participants at the *kire* workshops (who in other contexts might be called the 'beneficiaries' or the 'target group'); CEP facilitators and staff; government officials from the *woredas*, zone and region representatives of the donor organisation, SIDA. It was the intention of the design to involve people from all of these groups in the monitoring and analysis of information by (a) making selections of what they considered to be the most important changes occurring in active CEP *kires* during a particular reporting period and (b) then explaining the reasons for their choices.

In brief, the design of the monitoring process involves the following steps. Every level of the programme is asked to select what it considers to be the most important changes to have occurred in their particular geographical area during a specific reporting period. This begins at the *kire* level. The resulting selections are collected together with selections from other groups at the same level and then forwarded to the next level where the selection process is repeated. At every stage, only four selected changes are forwarded to the next level. The process moves from the *kires* through the *woredas* to the zone and finally to the region. Along with their selection, every group explains why they made the selections they did. After all selections and explanations have filtered their way up the monitoring system, explanations and reflections begin adjourned back down through the chain by memos and group discussions.

Building from the bottom-up, a minimum of 288 important changes are identified by *kire* participants during a single reporting period (4 changes x 6 *kires* x 3 facilitation units x 4 *woredas* based on work in the original four pilot *woredas*). From these, the selection process eventually results in 16 significant changes to be reviewed by the zonal steering committee. Explanations about the choices accompany every selective step.

In the beginning, facilitators tried to collect stories concerning three specific types of change: (a) changes in attitudes or images, (b) changes with regard to sustainable development, and (c) changes relative to physical or economic well-being. A fourth change was not stipulated which left its subject matter entirely open to the discretion of *kire* members. *Kire* participants at CPW follow-up meetings, however, found the different categories to be confusing and redundant and the facilitators had difficulty in explaining them. Disliking the awkwardness of the discussion, the facilitators began to give it slight attention or dropped it altogether from the agenda of the follow-up meetings.

Other problems were revealed, too, with the qualitative monitoring design during a review meeting with the Lead Facilitators in Dessie, 4–15 March 1996. One of the biggest was related to the involvement of *woreda* administrators and officials. They were confused by their role in the monitoring process and repeatedly expressed hesitation about deciding the importance of reported changes when they had not seen these changes with their own eyes. Reviewing unconfirmed stories and making judgements about them seemed to *woreda* personnel to be an empty gesture. After the first monitoring meeting, they were increasingly uninterested in participating in the exercise.

A lengthy discussion of these problems led to a number of modifications to the monitoring process. The categories of change were dropped; people were just asked to identify the changes they thought to be most important. The quarterly facilitator meetings became the primary occasion for consolidating stories from the *kires* and selecting the changes across the entire *woreda* which they thought to be most important. These stories were expanded to include changes observed among extension officers working the programme areas. *Woreda* officials were also asked to participate directly in verification trips.

After modifying the process, follow-up meetings with the *kires* included a review and discussion of the one story of change selected by *woreda* officials to be most significant. This took place at the end of the meeting and served as both 'feedback' and an opportunity for further reflection. After telling the story, the facilitators led a discussion with *kire* participants based on the following questions:

- What surprised you about this story?
- If you could ask questions of the actors in this story, what additional information would you like to have?
- In what ways do you think this story represents an important change (if you agree that it does represent an important change)?
- If something like the events reported in the story were to happen in this *kire*, what would you do the same and what would you do differently?
- How might such actions lead to an important change in this *kire*?

Then in conclusion, the participants were asked to identify the most important changes that had taken place in their *kire* as a result of activities associated with the programme.

What impact did this have on the *kires*? Debriefing sessions with the facilitators indicated that people were certainly interested in hearing what other *kires* had accomplished and what the *woreda* officials thought to be most important. The conversation also appeared often to spark the competitive spirit of *kire* members. After discussing the story, people were eager to explain their own accomplishments in doing self-reliant development. The facilitators also thought these discussions led to renewed decisions among the participants to assume responsibility for the new action plans they had just created earlier during the follow-up meeting. In a sense this was an attitude of 'if they can do it, we can do it better'!

Relative to the *woreda*, officials often approach their verification trips with scepticism. Though they had heard many interesting stories about change, they were not convinced that such things were really occurring. Once in the field, they were surprised by what they saw. To date, there have been no instances of these officials coming across false reports. Indeed, reports indicate that the *woreda* officials have repeatedly been surprised by the motivation, commitment and accomplishments of small local projects completed by *kire* members through the exclusive use of local resources and knowledge.

In conclusion, the qualitative monitoring of CEP, based on 'perceptions of change,' utilises a highly inductive approach in which unpredicted indicative events become the basis for drawing conclusions about results. This is valuable when programme objectives of 'empowerment' are often wrapped in ideas such as increased participation, self-confidence, responsibility, capacity for problem-solving, etc. Such conceptual categories are extremely difficult to evaluate. Rather than being confined to a narrow range of predetermined indicators, the CEP approach has the possibility of being flexible and adaptive to changing circumstances.

This is in sharp contrast, of course, to conventional monitoring approaches which are deductive in orientation, i.e., those that exist with a conception of a desired state and which then attempt to identify empirical indicators of its occurrence.

As the field experience indicates, the qualitative monitoring system employed by CEP practically reinforced power at the bottom and is an alternative to conventional approaches in which experts far from the field often define the monitoring subjects. It has given those closest to the experience being monitored the opportunity to guide the process by making their choices and interpretations at the beginning rather than at the end. Officials above are put into the position of responding to a diversity of explanations generated from below. Consistent with the aims of CEP as a whole, the basic monitoring agenda is thereby firmly set from the bottom rather than the top.

Chapter 5

Lessons from the Practice

In previous chapters we have seen that one of the great challenges confronting agencies relates to the need to bridge the gap between the rhetoric and the reality of impact assessment. The previous chapter provided examples of the case studies presented during the 1996 Workshop, illustrating some of the innovative practices which as yet have not entered mainstream literature. In this chapter, we analyse what these experiences provide in terms of lessons from the practice and try to move towards a conclusion and pointers for the future. As a basis for this chapter we have used the 46 or so different documents presented and discussed at or produced during the Workshop. Where appropriate specific documents and case studies are referred to otherwise the full list of material is included in Appendix 1.

In *Measuring the Process* (Marsden, Oakley and Pratt 1994) we shared the experiences of several agencies in trying to come to grips with the ways different methods could be or had been used in evaluating social development. Since writing this book we realised that although there is a growing body of experiences of using different methods there are still many problems confronting an agency wishing to evaluate the impact of their social development programme. There are certain elements where some of the theory needs to be tied more closely to the ways and means of operationalising ideas to the specifics of programme management, project cycles, and the differences in context and cultures. In this chapter we have tried to identify some of the main areas in which we think that there are general lessons to be learned about evaluations, especially related to evaluating impact.

RETHINKING APPROACHES TO EVALUATION

Evaluation as Process
If evaluation has traditionally had a bad name, and evaluators were regarded as the sector's assassins or policemen, some of the more recent practice has final-

ly tried to retrieve evaluation from the margins and return it to the centre of project life. In the world of international development it has taken a while to begin to counteract the negative image of evaluation, perhaps because of the inordinate dominance of the power imbalance between donors and recipients which no amount of discussion about partnership has been able to counteract. There is a growing school of thought which argues that the evaluation process should be a part of the process of social development itself. How can we expect communities or groups of people to engage in the long road to autonomous and sustainable development without them being included in the process of development through the cycle of action–reflection–action? We will talk more about 'participation' further in this chapter, as it is clear that the participation of different key stakeholders is essential both for social development itself and to evaluate the impact of social development programmes. Without the participation of a range of stakeholders it is unlikely that we will be able to evaluate impact, and many of the cases we reviewed point towards this conclusion. Agencies have demonstrated that it is essential to ensure that participation is a process which starts at the beginning and continues through the life of an intervention and beyond.

Evaluation is regarded by some agencies as a way of ensuring that communities become engaged in both the programme process as it directly effects them and in the wider process of agency strategic planning. It is then argued that in this manner the evaluation should benefit the communities engaged in the development activities thus moving beyond the concept of evaluation as only providing management information for managers to one of informing and assisting the primary stakeholders in the development process. As such it also becomes an instrument for mutual accountability which may mitigate the negative connotations referred to above and instead contribute to trust between participants.

> . . . evaluation may be understood as a resource that enables the NGOs and popular groups, to acknowledge their potentialities and deficiencies, contributing to the widening of its . . . capacities. (Bellicanta, Workshop Paper 12)

It has also been argued that evaluation can be used and indeed should be used to reinforce more positive approaches towards gender. Thus evaluations are seen as one way in which women can provide an input into programmes and counteract tendencies to ignore their interests and contributions. Traditional positivist evaluations are regarded as having reinforced incorrect or damaging gender stereotypes through not encompassing the full range of views and perceptions from both genders but merely reflecting the prejudices of programme planners, technicians and the more entrenched gender (usually male) interests (Walters, Workshop Paper 19). The experience of an alternative client-based approach to evaluation is growing. Development workers are beginning to value an approach which provides them with a range of views from different stakeholders. Where the commitment to listening to clients is sincere and the methods used are appropriate, we are witnessing more development agencies recognising the value of an approach which is responsive to their clients or beneficiaries, including exciting work with children as well as adults (Boyden and Ennew 1997).

Pluralism

If there is one thing which has become increasingly clear since the first workshop on evaluating social development in 1989, it is that good evaluation must encompass as many stakeholders as possible. Where we introduced the concept of the interpretative evaluation to development agencies through the 1989 Workshop, we now see large numbers of agencies attempting exercises based on a cross-section of perceptions from different stakeholders. This is starkly contrasted to the 'positivistic' tradition of trying to seek a unitary set of objective truths about a set of social processes, often packaged into a development project. An increasing number of agencies have argued for a pluralist approach which entails using different methods to ensure a representation of the views of different stakeholders. Ideally with primary stakeholders identifying the objectives of development interventions as well as the indicators for monitoring and evaluation. They also recognise that the methods used may well vary according to the stakeholder and their own cultural, social or professional context. Thus we see evaluations which incorporate the views of 'beneficiaries or clients' through focus group discussions, alongside formal interviews with key people such as the local bishop or government representative. There are sometimes problems in relying on a stakeholder-based approach in ensuring that the 'primary' stakeholders remain the priority group in the process, and where there are conflicts between major stakeholders. But overall the stakeholder approach has more than proved its worth.

Practice suggests that we need first to be clear who the stakeholders actually are, and several relatively simple techniques have been developed to allow us to do this. Some use a matrix system based on that illustrated in *Measuring the Process*, others have relied on initial workshops of some key players to identify those other stakeholders whose views need to be incorporated into the evaluation. One of the consequences of the introduction of stakeholder analysis is the inclusion of the views from those not originally anticipated to be a part of or affected by a programme. When managed well it also becomes a way of ensuring that the client comes first, and helps counteract the tendency of development programmes to be run more for the convenience of the agency staff and donors rather than for the clients or beneficiaries.

As our experience grows and this approach matures it becomes more evident that pluralism does not mean that all opinions are equally valid; what it does mean is that each group or individual will hold opinions which should be recorded. It is important that we permit these views to be aired and that they are not suppressed. We may find some of these personally unacceptable but surely it is better to know that a certain group still holds such views rather than ignore their existence. In less extreme cases, agencies have been able to use an evaluation to highlight the differences of opinion and perspective between stakeholders as a way of opening a debate, discussion and process of negotiation between them. As such the evaluation plays an important role in assisting the different actors to see themselves within the wider context.

If the practice tells us anything it is that to evaluate social development we need to have a pluralist approach which encompasses the widest range of stakeholders, but which clearly prioritises the client. If we are not putting the client first we are probably failing in our prime reason for existing as development agencies. Further it becomes clear that such a client-based approach can only succeed if the donor is no longer the prime driving force and recipient of the evaluation. It also becomes clear that evaluation must be regarded as something integral to the development process which helps rather than hinders community/group participation in this process and brings gender relations to the fore rather than ignore or deny their existence. In those cases we reviewed where some of these principles have been observed, we begin to see the evaluation genuinely becoming a part of the process of social development and providing a mechanism for negotiation between stakeholders.

THE PARTICIPATORY BASIS FOR EVALUATION

There is a great deal of ideology surrounding the concept of participation, much of which does little to help us as development practitioners. Recent experience has, however, been more useful in clarifying what we mean by participation and its qualities. Rather than regard participation as a stand-alone concept we now need to have a more sophisticated approach which defines levels and forms of participation in a context-specific manner. One way we have tried to do this is by treating participation as a spectrum and then relating it to the programme cycle thus providing a bench-mark against which we can assess it. This draws upon several earlier attempts, such as the 'ladders of participation' elaborated by certain authors but which we tie to a project cycle which represents to a large extent the reality within which many practitioners are obliged to work. The example of levels of participation given in Table 5.1 ranges from merely **informing** people through to self-management by beneficiaries. Thus some agencies feel that by informing people that an evaluation is happening they have sufficiently brought them into the process; whereas the next stage is considered to be one of **consultation** where at least views are sought but no more. **Active involvement** is where the level of participation is stepped up to the degree to which people have more than a passive role although the process is still driven by others. When we talk of people **assuming responsibility** we refer to a significantly increased degree of participation whereby people are setting agendas and in terms of evaluation are driving the process for their own needs rather than just fulfilling obligations to external bodies such as donors. The final category of **self-management** would encompass groups originating and managing a process of evaluation as a part of their own needs and management. Underlying this whole process is an assumption that the agency has a stable and mature relationship with the communities with which it works as a precondition for meaningful participation.

Table 5.1 Project Cycle and Participation

	Inform	Consult	Active involvement	Assuming responsibility	Self-management
Needs assessment					
Design					
Planning					
Implementation					
Monitoring					
Evaluation and impact assessment					

On the other axis, the categories will vary according to the agency. Here we have a stylised project/programme management cycle running from needs assessment, design, planning through implementation to monitoring and finally to evaluation and impact assessment. It is recognised that the degree of participation at each stage may well vary considerably and need not be uniform for all programmes. It should be noted, however, that it would not be realistic to expect very high levels of participation in an evaluation of a programme which previously demonstrated very low levels of participation in the earlier stages of the project cycle.

In practice several people have argued that the art is to maintain the flexibility in programmes which permit genuine participation but without sacrificing accountability. The way this balance is carried out will in part depend upon the degree of flexibility from the donor and their acceptance of alternative methods. This tension between some of the more formalistic procedures and techniques now being promoted, especially by donor agencies, and the need for a flexibility which can allow people to develop their own methods and ways of evaluating is at the heart of debates in many agencies. Some find that they need to undergo an exercise which clarifies the stages in their project cycle where participation is possible and those where due to other obligations (legal requirements, auditors' demands, official limitations on government departments) the potential for participation is constrained. If these restrictions are real rather than the product of bureaucratic convenience they should be made explicit in a transparent manner and where possible ways found of overcoming the constraints on participation.

In reviewing the examples presented at the November Workshop it would appear that although many agencies are moving in the direction of more participatory evaluations and have been able to introduce methods which increase stakeholder participation, few demonstrate very high levels of participation. In other words, referring to Table 5.1, few of the experiences can be said to have been driven by clients, most are still the product of the external agent providing other stakeholders with the opportunity to participate and let their views be heard. While examples of the use of what are now termed PRA methods, are common as ways of obtaining information and views, there are less examples of client driven or self-evaluation despite some earlier work in the late 1980s (Feuerstein 1986). Perhaps the emphasis on introducing methods which enable greater participation is as much as we have a right to expect given the previous long history of top-down development. Progress has been and is being made by many agencies as they seek to improve the levels and nature of participation and move along the matrix presented above.

REDISCOVERY OF THE BASELINE

There was a time when development workers argued against the whole notion of a baseline and claimed that providing one was a practical impossibility and not even necessary. It was felt that ethically the idea of collecting a great deal of information was doubtful in situations where people's needs were so many and so evident. What changed this attitude, or at least is changing it, is twofold: first the realisation that many needs assessments were wrong and secondly the desire to evaluate impact.

One of the great contributions of PRA has been to open up the debate about the very poor level of needs assessment in development programmes. PRA techniques have led to a fundamental questioning of many areas of development where previously 'professional' opinions of outsiders were always given priority over those of local people, including clients. Old assumptions have been challenged and other movements, such as the push towards greater awareness of gender and generational differences for example, have assisted the recognition that needs assessments should also start with the people involved (Chambers 1997; Moser 1991; Boyden and Ennew 1997). Therefore, what was seen as an unnecessary luxury becomes a prime stage in any development programme. For it becomes essential now to carry out participatory appraisals in order to gain greater insights into needs and to explore different ideas which can be the basis for programming. In terms of the debate over baselines this should mean more material of different types against which we can evaluate the development interventions themselves. At the moment many people are trying to use PRA-type techniques retrospectively as we shall see elsewhere, although for many reasons this is fraught with difficulties. It is to be hoped that improved needs assessments and appraisals will provide the baselines for future evaluations although it is still too early for many of these developments to come to fruition. There continue to be problems in understanding and factoring into impact assessment other external influences and in proving the cause–effect relationship.

The second resurgence of interest in providing baselines comes from the attempts at gauging the impact of social development programmes which have consistently run into problems because of the lack of comparative data due to the absence of any form of baseline survey. Where baseline material does exist it is often at the level of very basic physical data taken from official figures (immunisation rates, literacy rates) not disaggregated down to the level of the 'target' group of the intervention. A strong message from most sources is that without some form of baseline it is not really possible to assess impact. Furthermore, it is argued that given the need for qualitative material to assess impact it is even more important that the baseline goes beyond the minimalist physical indicators. Qualitative indicators are considered essential because impact is about change over time and social development assumes change to be its focus. So much of the change we are trying to assess has to do with the qualitative rather than the quantitative nature of socio-economic relations.

There is an alternative to either having to start with a comprehensive baseline, or being dependent upon a totally retrospective attempt at assessing impact. The idea of a 'rolling baseline' has gained popularity amongst practitioners although in 'scientific' or 'statistical' terms it may not meet certain standards of rigour. The idea of the rolling baseline is to turn the material collected through monitoring into the baseline for future activities. An example of this was provided in the CINDE case study of a pre-school education programme in chapter 3 of *Measuring the Process*: group 'A' joins the programme, while setting up activities the group carries out its own assessment of where they think their children have educational needs, the teachers and other staff make their own assessment and the progress of this group is monitored in this fashion over time. Later when groups 'B' to 'X' join the programme assessments are similarly made of the groups and the children which can be compared to group 'A' both as it was when it joined the programme and how it is now after several years within the programme. This should reveal how group 'A' has changed and also provide a 'control group' to the extent that we can compare the later groups which join the scheme to how group 'A' originally was when it joined. Any marked differences between the status of groups joining at different times may highlight changes in the wider society (for example, the introduction of a state pre-school scheme) unrelated to the programme. Clearly not all groups are totally comparable and not all differences can be explained by the programme activities, but this system does give us a basis for comparisons and provides data over time without an excessive initial investment establishing baselines and control groups. It provides sufficient information for our purposes which do not require one hundred per cent statistical validity. Indeed some argue that we should be questioning strict definitions of statistical rigour (Pretty 1994).

An alternative to using a baseline is provided by some of the examples of retrospective impact assessment such as those from Ghana and Zimbabwe given in Boxes 5.1 and 5.2. However, as the Zimbabwean case shows there may well be problems in trying to reconstruct the history of a programme and the Ghana case illustrates the resources required to carry out such methods.

One final warning which several have voiced about putting together the baseline relates to the question of 'whose reality counts', to steal a phrase from Robert Chamber's (1997) latest book. In entering the exercise for establishing a baseline there is a danger of deciding for people what material should be collected, which questions to ask, which priority areas to focus the research on. Who decides the answers to these and other related questions can affect the outcomes of the whole process not only of setting the baseline but of later devel-

Box 5.1   Ghana: A Retrospective Example

'It was also recognised that it is not always possible or desirable (even if methodologically simpler) to fix indicators of poverty at the beginning of a process and track these same indicators over time. In fact how people's own indicators of poverty change over time is an important element in understanding how their needs, attitudes and values are shifting' (Kamara and Roche, Workshop Paper 41).

Therefore ISODEC explained that in their programme they used the joint collection of data with different stakeholders and secondary materials and results of participatory organisational assessments to create a baseline for the region in which they worked. They included in this a retrospective participatory village assessment using 6–8 villages and samples for more in-depth studies to review recent changes which both contributed to the assessment of the impact of agency interventions and provided material for a baseline for future assessments. Some of the sample families were chosen for longer-term tracking of change alongside a mixture of techniques such as time-lines, institutional mapping, seasonal calendars, well-being ranking, and expenditure analysis. But lessons from these exercises were that:

- time and resources are required;
- it is possible to borrow from the experiences and existing literature and then on the basis of this to innovate and adapt ideas to a specific context;
- it is important to develop the local capacity to accompany such exercises while also seeking external assistance; and
- most importantly this sort of programme requires trust on all sides.

opment programmes. We need to be conscious of imposing our ideas of what constitutes priorities, the data to be collected and the changes required. If we are to avoid this we must be aware of the need to capture the views, opinions and perceptions of local people through our work. These will be the basis of much of our later monitoring and evaluation and eventually our attempt to review impact through changes as reflected by the primary actors' perceptions of these changes in their own lives.

MEASURING QUALITATIVE CHANGE

The ACTIONAID case study from Nepal arrived at a pertinent conclusion that where they had used both quantitative methods (large survey) and qualitative methods (case studies, unstructured interviews, focus group discussions), the quantitative studies provided information on project outcomes but not impact. The impact data was obtained from the qualitative study which showed the felt and observed changes in the quality of life (Singh et al., Workshop Paper 32). They concluded that possibly only qualitative data could therefore provide information on impact. Elsewhere, in *Measuring the Process* and Chapters 2 and 3 above, we have noted that the earlier polarisation between quantitative and qualitative methods was based on certain false dichotomies. Both can have uses in specific contexts.

Box 5.2 ACTIONAID Nepal

ACTIONAID tried to combine quantitative and qualitative methods in an impact assessment in Nepal. The quantitative survey used indicators identified several years previously (see Chapter 4.2) and led to an extensive survey of 600 households and a sample of schoolchildren. The qualitative was based on a sample of villages (clusters) utilising PRA-type methods. To back this up a set of case studies was also prepared at the level of individuals, families, groups and villages. Some of the lessons included:

- The problem of moving goal posts. The old baseline no longer seemed relevant to current programmes and the new methods were not producing data comparable with the old statistics collected by the older methods, so there were several incomplete sets of incomparable data.
- The question arose, were they assessing impact against yesterday's goals or today's?
- The quantitative material revealed more about outcomes than impact; the qualitative more about changes in the quality of life and therefore more about impact.
- There was still a felt need to understand more about the 'intra-household changes', for example effects on women and children rather than assume household or community as single units. Thus the data tended to show more about change for the overall community and less about the individual level.

(Singh et al., Workshop Paper 32)

Neither is it the case that the qualitative cannot be measured, and there are many well tried ways of putting qualitative indicators into a measurable form (Marsden et al. 1994). One is by asking people what they consider would be an indicator of the change that they wish to see. Later evaluations can review progress against that indicator as well as ask the question again of the same group. It is also possible to repeat the question by asking the group what is the indicator they would now identify as illustrating the changes that have occurred. Adding numbers to such replies is not difficult. Once one accepts that people's views have a validity in an evaluation then the artificial distinction between hard and soft numbers becomes irrelevant. If in addition one uses for validation the method of triangulation of data collected by different methods, one can have considerable confidence in the information despite the lack of statistical significance.

Where many evaluations run into difficulty is not in the issue of turning qualitative indicators into numerical form. The rather more difficult issue is how to measure attitudinal change. Possibly changes in behaviour can act as a proxy for attitudes; for example, more girls being educated as an increasing awareness of their human and social value. Or, the increased demand for contraceptives as a proxy to changing attitudes to family size. But not all links between behaviour and attitudes will be apparent. It will sometimes be difficult to disentangle the tangible results (girls with schooling earn more) from the intangible (educated girls have more self-confidence and are more emancipated). Of course we can ask people what they think about certain issues, practices and behaviour; changes in their answers may reflect a major change in attitudes. But how do we know whether they have amended their behaviour accordingly or is it all rhetoric to meet the new orthodoxy? The answer to this last question probably lies in a mixture of choosing the right questions and cross-checking information.

One risk in relying entirely on the perceptions from people affected by a programme is that these change anyway and not always in the most obvious ways. For example, a good social development programme may, and probably should, raise people's expectations both of themselves and the outside world. As awareness increases so will their self-confidence of what they can achieve and their expectations of those around them including project workers. It is not unusual to find people being more critical of a programme once it is up and running, not because the programme is doing less well but because it has helped people to achieve an awareness that yet more could be done with and for them. It would be unfortunate if an evaluation were to penalise programme staff when the resulting changed responses from people were in fact a sign of their heightened awareness and confidence resulting from the programme. Therefore, many programmes have instituted validation exercises, sometimes using group workshops, at other times through peer or expert (key informant) interviews with close but external observers, to obtain their views on the changes as reported by those involved. Such peer interviews can provide a second level of checks on the initial perception interviews and exercises to validate what people are saying and to avoid the sort of problem described above.

There will probably always be changes which defeat attempts to collate them in a simple numerical manner but where qualitative methods can still provide us with the spirit of these changes. In the last analysis, people and the communities in which they live are not homogeneous and we should not expect totally uniform results from all those involved in social development any more than we expect to see all members of a given society with identical characteristics.

TRYING TO UNDERSTAND CHANGE

If we agree that impact assessment is all about measuring the change which has resulted from an external developmental intervention then we find ourselves caught against the problem of causality. Can we over time be certain that changes are the result of our intervention or a consequence of other factors completely outside of our programme?

The first thing we must do is to scan the external environment. Many agencies are not well geared to understanding what is happening outside their own walls. They still, despite so many lessons to the contrary, treat their 'projects' as isolated, stand-alone entities devoid of external contact and influence. In a rapidly changing world we cannot afford to ignore the effects of external influences. Whether it is an issue of the government changing prices of basic goods and thus reducing the profitability of small farmers or changes in the law regarding women's property, the truth is that there are a myriad of factors which can support or undermine our development objectives. Being aware of these externalities should be a part of good monitoring as well as a key element in evaluation of both outcomes and impact. Scanning such factors as social, economic, political and cultural help identify external causes of change, as well as methods such as critical event analysis of major events such as drought, flood, fire, etc. may identify other factors which may have an impact on a group of people and the development interventions with them.

Box 5.3 Zimbabwe: Retrospective Assessment

Novib and OXFAM UK/I have tried to tackle the problem of assessing
impact in the absence of a strong baseline through retrospectively constructing events, described as 'the next best approach'. They have done this
through reviewing implementation (monitoring) reports and asking people
to recall the recent history of a project and related events within the context
of the project. This method it was hoped would make it possible to identify explanations for particular events or decisions that may have influenced
the impact of the project. It was recognised that this is not an ideal
approach, but that a 'reconstructed history' may be all that is possible.
Some of the early examples of such retrospective assessment shows the
many practical problems. Thus ENDA's attempt to do this for several projects in Zimbabwe found that they were unable to overcome the poor previous record-keeping of the programmes and that they also were unable to
obtain the assistance of the previous staff of the programmes who were
unwilling often to be interviewed and help reconstruct the programme. In
programmes with better prior monitoring and other records it has to be seen
whether this method is able as a second best to provide the sort of impact
assessment we are looking for.

(Es, Neggers and Blankenberg, Workshop Paper 43; Sola, Workshop Paper
38)

Secondly to review causality we must have some form of baselines; although
some agencies are exploring retrospective impact assessment, others have not
found this very satisfactory in the absence of a baseline. With a baseline we are
able to know what change has occurred in the time frame. Moreover, if we have
some form of control group we can learn how our intervention has assisted the
groups with which we work compared to others, and are thus able to see how
much is merely a part of a general trend. It also means that we can allow for and
adjust our findings for negative general trends, not just those which are positive. In other words we need to know not only that all indicators in an area are
positive (and therefore that perhaps the claims made by a programme exagger-
ate its own importance), but also the reverse. For example, a programme may
appear not to have improved people's lives very much, but if the general economic context has deteriorated greatly, then the programme may have mitigat-
ed an even worse decline suffered by the populace at large.

Thirdly, as noted above, we must include in our impact assessment the views
and opinions of the main stakeholders. It is through the qualitative views of

stakeholders and asking them about the changes as they perceive them that we can start to build up our picture of change. Through such an approach we also identify the unexpected consequences of the programme, whether positive or negative, which in the longer term may be quite significant. Most development programmes will not be big enough to affect entire nations, such that even the largest will still be small scale and partial in coverage in comparison to the totality of the influences on the lives of people. Large-scale surveys including market surveys, and mass statistical exercises are unlikely to provide sufficiently disaggregated data to show how a specific intervention has an impact on people in the longer term. We are more likely to be able to bring together a picture of change over time and relate this to specific interventions through alternative methods such as 'perception' interviews and group discussions, in which simple questions are asked about changes in one's lifetime, changes in one's life compared to one's parents and how a particular project has assisted individuals.

One problem which is hard to overcome is the fact that we are still so constrained by the concept of the project, usually two to three years with a start and finish. Life bears little relationship to the project cycle we have invented for ourselves. The point here is that we find ourselves looking at projects as though they existed as a fixed reality in time and space rather than a form of payment for a set of activities. Although we all know that most projects exist merely as a packaging or repackaging of a set of activities for a specific donor we persist with the myth that this is not the case. From the point of view of evaluation we are unlikely to get a clear idea of outcomes if we adhere to this myth and will definitely not get an idea of impact. We must take a view of the entire set of interventions in an area by the agency or group of agencies if we are to obtain a true picture of both the inputs into a community as well as the outcomes and impact. Although we will also have to face the constraints imposed on us by the project funding framework in which we are obliged to work and find compromises between the holistic and partial perspectives. Indeed there is still plenty to do to improve impact assessment at the project level despite its limitations.

Many agencies may well have supported several consecutive projects with a group over many years and it makes little sense to treat each project as a discrete entity. It should be the impact of the overall set of interventions for which we should be looking if we are to make any sense of the totality. Often the projects may well have changed over time, with different emphases, driving ideologies and focus as trends change or the group itself evolves. We see so many areas which have started with traditional external inputs (building of a school, dispensary staffed by nuns) moving through an emphasis on agriculture through new technologies (seeds, fertilisers), then onto village development committees and formal 'institution building' and then perhaps to a focus on widening village participation to all members of the community (women, children, outcasts, landless, etc.). To gauge impact the entire set of interventions is likely to be relevant not just the one funded by the donor requesting the evaluation.

One of the problems we have encountered is the very small number of *post hoc* evaluations that are carried out some time after the departure of a development agency. There still seems to be a reluctance or an inability to revisit areas well after the end of a programme in order to carry out an impact assessment or evaluation. The examples we reviewed of impact assessment were mainly of programmes which were still running. Those carried out by ENDA Zimbabwe were of programmes completed a couple of years previously and this may explain why they had problems using the retrospective technique in the absence of good baseline data and deficiencies in basic project documentation, including monitoring. This made the retrospective technique less than perfect given the reluctance of some ex-staff to be interviewed and other problems. Possibly with better pre-existing data they might have been able to piece together enough to then be able to attempt a more informed assessment but without this they were unhappy with the resulting studies (Sola, Workshop Paper 38).

If donors really want to support improved impact studies there would be a strong argument in favour of funding such longitudinal studies *post hoc* to gain more insight into the degree to which impacts have been longer term and sustainable after the departure of development agencies. Possibly a random sampling of development programmes might be useful and honest, or selecting a few and investing in better appraisal, monitoring and evaluation to ensure that materials would be available to a future generation of evaluators looking at long-term impact.

CULTURE

An important area which is beginning to emerge from the practice relates to the cultural context in which different methods may work, and where they may or may not be acceptable. The evidence is still not clear enough to be certain of the positive or constraining nature of different methods and approaches. Anecdotes and experience would indicate a future fertile area of study. For example, our own work has illustrated massive problems in parts of Latin America when we have tried to ask questions about the sources of income and expenditure in NGOs; this should not be a surprise in those countries with no tradition or legal obligation to provide audited accounts for public consumption. In South Asia alternatively the culture of public accountability is such that similar questions are unlikely to be met with any problems, while questions relating to leadership styles and hierarchical structures will often not be well received.

Another important area which possibly is culturally determined relates to the acceptability of the group versus the individual and vice versa. In some cultures evaluators are often surprised by what can and cannot be asked either in group discussions or with individuals. In Northern Europe questions of a personal nature are probably best kept to an individual interview, whereas some evaluators have found that in some cultures this can be seen as more threatening than a group discussion of the same subject. There is also an assumption implicit in many evaluations that the group perspective is more accurate and acceptable than the individual. This assumption has yet to be tested. It is not at all clear that in all circumstances what a group publicly can agree on is as accurate as the compilation of individuals' views gathered separately. We have all experienced individuals agreeing with a 'group consensus' in public while arguing something very different in private. The practice would indicate the need to use both sets of approach, individual and group, and cross-check the results for agreements and discrepancies.

CONTEXT

There are two key points which have arisen regarding the context in which development programmes work. The first is that regular scanning is essential. The second is that what many agencies regard as externalities may in truth be at the heart of a social development programme.

The need for regular external scanning is essential at all stages of a programme from the initial needs assessment through design, implementation, monitoring and evaluation of both outputs and impact. Many NGOs find it hard to believe that this is something they need to be concerned about, until the external environment impinges strongly upon their lives. Whether this be in the form of a change in government or legislation, or in terms of factors directly affecting their programme such as price changes, we ignore the external at our peril. The same holds for other 'official' programmes which can as easily fall into the trap of ignoring external factors. In terms of the project cycle, only with external mapping can we offset biases for or against the project: whether things would have improved regardless of the intervention, or conversely deteriorated may be entirely due to major external forces which need to be factored into the evaluation.

Many argued during the Workshop that the socio-economic-political contexts in which development agencies worked should not be treated as secondary factors during the process of evaluating impact. The context in which many of us work should be treated as being at the very heart of social development. Examples were provided of severe cases of income inequality, of state failure to provide basic services to the general population, of undemocratic decision-making over resources to the detriment of the poor. Social development was seen as having these and other social injustices as the prime rather than secondary focus of its concern and work. It was thought that to disassociate the crucial context in which we worked from the evaluation of impact, could undermine and undervalue the longer-term goals and aspirations of those working in social development and hence whether they were indeed having the impact for which they were striving. It was therefore concluded that impact assessment must take full account of the bigger picture in arriving at a conclusion about the success or failure of social development in making real changes to people's lives.

FUTURE DIRECTIONS: TOWARDS A CONCLUSION

In the present chapter we have outlined certain lessons which we believe have emerged from recent practice in the area of evaluating the impact of social development. It would be foolhardy to pretend that all of the many problems which have confronted practitioners, as opposed to theorists, have been resolved. Before arriving at a conclusion it might be worth revisiting the journey we have been on as reflected by the previous chapters.

In the Introduction we described the journey, starting in the mid-1980s with concerns about what appeared to be the dominant paradigm of development and the way it was being monitored and evaluated. As a reaction to this positivist approach the first International Workshop on Evaluating Social Development was held in 1989 which for most development workers introduced a series of key concepts, previously not in common use. Key words, such as negotiation, pluralism, people-centred evaluation, began to enter our thinking and practice. Simultaneously a great deal of work in areas such as participatory development, participatory analysis and others were showing the way to a new approach to development. Some of the practical aspects of turning these and related concepts into practice were the focus of the second Workshop in 1992. At that time INTRAC started to run courses in monitoring and evaluation primarily for European-based relief and development agencies, using the concepts and material from these workshops.

Initially we found that we were introducing ideas which went very much against the orthodoxy adopted by official donors which was a very mechanical interpretation of results-based management, including monitoring and evaluation. During the past five years we have noticed a marked change, however, such that many agencies not only no longer find our approach alien but have gone a long way towards accepting these ideas and adapting them to their needs. The third Workshop shared some of the new innovations and experiments in a people-centred participatory approach to impact assessment and we have sought to capture some of these in this book. Looking to the future we expect and hope to witness even more imaginative but rigorous programmes assessing the impact of social development.

Chapter 1 sought to revisit the concept of social development, clearly placing words such as social change and transformation back at the centre of this concept, and linked approach to development. The chapter traced the history of social development and the way in which the concept was rescued away from a move towards being a purely mechanical delivery of a package of social welfare and other services. Chapter 2 charted the progress of evaluating social development for the majority of people and agencies. As such we presented uncritically the contemporary status quo. In Chapter 3 we moved towards examining some of the ways different groups of agencies have tried to develop their own approach to impact assessment through, for example, designing information systems. In that chapter we were able to move towards some conclusions based on the material collected since 1992 and from the conference of 1996. These included the basic principle that the approach to monitoring and evaluation should be 'minimum but effective'. To be effective there must be a recognisable 'system' but one which is flexible and adaptable to the needs of the main actors or stakeholders, and which does not cripple the project itself. In Chapter 4 we explored some of the specific examples presented to the 1996 Workshop by agencies themselves, and from this were able to review some of the attempts to 'close the gap between rhetoric and reality' in the evaluation of social development. Earlier in the current chapter we then spelled out the lessons learned through the review of practice as a way of identifying some of the key areas which must be dealt with by agencies seeking to carry out an impact assessment.

Throughout this book it should be clear that there is at the present time a tension or dichotomy between one major trend which is towards greater accountability to 'clients' or intended beneficiaries on the one hand and to tighter, more systematic systems of accountability to donors on the other hand. We have always felt that the two forms of accountability can coexist. What is less clear is whether the methodologies used in pursuit of these two aims are always compatible. Certain donor conditionalities on the use of formats such as the logical framework do not help those agencies trying to remain flexible in developing new forms of impact assessment. We need to explain to and persuade donors that they need to be flexible in their own procedures to enable agencies genuinely and honestly to try to develop new forms of monitoring and evaluation and impact assessment. Indeed one could almost argue that they should be more concerned with auditing the information system rather than be the products of the system in terms of formal reporting. Key questions then cover both the detail of the micro-management of a project and whose interests the system best serves, what are the levels of needs for information from the various stakeholders, are they all being met and is the system skewed to only one set of stakeholders (commonly the donor).

Box 5.4 General Lessons on Methods for Impact Assessment

1. Put the client first.
2. No single method should have a monopoly of use.
3. Best use is to mix and match methods according to needs and group.
4. Attain a wide spread of perceptions from different stakeholders.
5. Participatory, qualitative methods help improve our understanding of impact.
6. Retrospective methods can provide some data; not ideal but better than nothing.
7. Need baseline, control groups, good appraisal, needs assessment to be certain of impact assessment.
8. It is hard to do impact assessment without prior information (either from a baseline or monitoring, project files, clear objectives, etc.).
9. Participatory methods need facilitation skills.
10. Analysis of data is crucial. Who does the analysis? Different stakeholders should be brought into this.
11. Participatory methods are not the same as a totally participatory process.
12. Time is required to gain trust and get into process evaluation.
13. It may be better to separate impact assessment from normal PME as these procedures/approaches are often not conducive to impact assessment.
14. Objectives must be clear at level of output, effects and impact.
15. Be firm in pushing forward with the impact assessment despite opposition and difficulties.
16. Cross-check information from different methods.
17. Keep the system as simple as possible without sacrificing accountability to both the client and the donor.

In Box 5.4 we have summarised some of the lessons learned from the practice; there are many more in the text of both this and previous chapters. There is one conclusion which we did not expect to emerge from the Workshop and which is unlikely to be popular with those many donor agencies who have tied their futures to an approach that stresses the monitoring and evaluation of observable outcomes.

In summary, we believe that the evidence shows that many of the methods which have been introduced as aids to programme planning, design, management, monitoring and evaluation are probably not useful in evaluating impact. These methods (such as logical frameworks) have a value in some of the programme stages mentioned but they fall short of informing us of programme impact. At best they may well provide an improved system of monitoring and may enable us to evaluate outputs and activities to the degree that they have been delivered to whom and at what cost. But these same methods are inadequate for relating what their impact has been on the client population.

Some of the cases reviewed such as ACTIONAID Nepal quoted above discussed some of the problems of living with the two approaches and making the best of it by trying to use both in order to provide a composite picture of impact. Others have retrospectively tried to reconstruct history through a menu of methods in part because the existing methods of monitoring and evaluation were not providing information on impact. What appears to emerge from these examples is that if we are serious about measuring impact the best way forward may not be to abolish the existing objective and outputs focused methods but to design a parallel system for assessing impact which runs independent of, but is linked to, the existing planning, monitoring and evaluation (PME) system. It will seem to be heresy to some but most of the practice we have surveyed indicates that most PME systems are better at assessing the activities and direct outputs of programmes than they are at assessing impact. Possibly this is why there is little material on impact and solid evaluations of impact are still relatively few, and why those who have attempted such exercises find themselves either without the appropriate data or engaged in historical retrospective studies. It will be difficult for agencies who have committed themselves to results based methods and logical frameworks to accept that what they are doing does not provide information on impact and that further and different methods need to be introduced or accepted into their horizons.

The conclusion we have reached is that the solution is to design a system specifically to assess impact, and that this should be done at the beginning of a project or programme's life so as to make the most of efforts around creating a baseline, establishing needs and initial perceptions, as well as possible indicators for change. Then as more traditional PME systems are operationalised to ensure accountability and efficiency of use of resources, a separate set of exercises can obtain the qualitative and other data on impact. The two exercises will cross over as they use each others' data – as we would want to avoid duplication – but they do constitute separate exercises to the extent that their focus is different. One has more to do with the way an agency uses resources, the other has more to do with the ultimate benefits gained by the clients. The two are not necessarily synonymous despite the assumption by many development workers and agencies that if resources are well used and if an agency follows a plan as predicted, then the clients will automatically benefit.

Looking to the future some of the more productive attempts to assess impact have recognised that to do so will require a real commitment from the sponsoring agency to a set of methods which are likely to be participatory in essence, with the client's needs and perceptions as their basis. Whether through retrospective means or through the initiation of impact assessment methods early in a programm's history we expect to see some challenging findings beginning to emerge from several agencies.

We set out to bridge the gap between the rhetoric and the reality of evaluating social development – there is still a huge amount to be done to completely fulfil this aim. Nevertheless, we believe that a great deal of progress has now been made since this series of international workshops started, with concepts which were alien to most of us now in common usage. An increasing number of exciting and productive initiatives are genuinely placing the new approach to the evaluation of social development back into the heart of development through the participation of people affected by development as well as improvement in the effectiveness of development interventions.

POSTSCRIPT: WHAT NEXT?

As we finally go to publication, a year after the Third International Workshop which brought together the people and ideas which inspired this book, we are asked what next. Many ideas will continue to develop on their own and in some of the agencies which have participated in the last Workshop. Other initiatives that have already been spawned out of the Workshop include a Web site called MandE News which was set up by individuals who participated in the Workshop as an attempt to capture more of the experimentation at a field level. Sources such as PLA Notes from IIED continue to provide a forum for field notes on participatory approaches. At the training level INTRAC continues to provide training programmes primarily for NGOs in various aspects of monitoring and evaluation. We also intend to assist more agencies to develop coherent, participatory systems which will allow them to improve both ongoing monitoring and evaluation and specifically the assessment of impact, through an action research programme over the next few years. We will also follow up suggestions from participants at the last Workshop for regional meetings to share specific experiences within certain regional contexts. It is hoped that the results from these, the action research and other initiatives could then feed into the

Fourth International Workshop on Evaluating Social Development planned for 1999. In the meantime we all look forward to hearing from individuals and groups about their experiences.

Appendix 1

Workshop Papers and Presentations

1. Dharam Ghai, 'Keynote Address'.

2. Max van den Berg, 'Impact Evalution of Social Development'.

3. Frances O'Gorman, 'Five Points for Reflection on Micro Base Community Experiences in Brazil'.

4. Caroline Harper, 'Reviewing Social Development'.

5. Peter Oakley, 'Overview Paper. Evaluationg Social Development: Outcomes and Impact'.

6. Anne Coles, 'Output to Purpose Reviews in ODA'.

7. Md. Shahabuddin, 'Agency Framework of Monitoring and Evaluation in Social Development: A Case of PROSHIKA'.

8. Hugh Goyder, 'ACTIONAID's Approach to Monitoring and Evaluation'.

9. Michael Edwards, 'NGO Performance: What Breeds Success? A Study of Approaches to Work in South Asia'.

10. Ali Abuel Gasim, 'Role of Community Participation in the Effectiveness of Development Projects'.

11. Cor Van Beuningen and Babara Does, 'Social Development or Sociocide? Object, Design and Evaluation of a Development Cooperation Project'.

12. Maria Lucia Bellicanta, 'Evaluation: Reflections over a Practice'.

13. Kees Biekart, 'Assessing Impact of Private Aid Interventions Aimed at Strengthening Political Roles in Civil Society'.

14. Claudia Fumo, 'The Contribution of NGO's to Development Effectiveness in World Bank-Supported Projects'.

15. Community Action Abroard, 'Indigenous Australia Programme'.

16. Elizabeth Wade-Brown, 'Evaluation Process and Methodology in CAFOD'.

17. Karin Stahl, 'Participatory Approaches to Evaluation – Experiences in Latin America'.

18. Ann Maria Philippi, Pedro Mege and Patricio Toledo, 'Community Evaluation as a Component of Organisational Development'.

19. Hettie Walters, 'Evaluation of Social Development from a Gender Perspective'.

20. Bernadette Kyany'a, 'Measuring Impact of Social Development Programmes: A Case Study from Botswana'.

21. Binoy Acharya, 'Evaluating Social Development Projects: Revisiting the Issue of Partnership'.

22. Helen Wedgwood and Alex Bush, 'ITDG's Experience of Participatory Evaluation Oriented Monitoring Systems (POEMS) in the International Food Programme'.

23. SNV, 'Group Dynamics as a Means to the Ongoing and Internal Evaluation of Social Change'.

24. Martin Dütting, 'The Project, Impact and Strategic Orientation on the Evolution of Misereor's Evaluation Work'.

25. Laura Renshaw and Richard Chase Smith, 'Politics and Process: Evaluating Economical Initiatives in the Amazon'.

26. Terry Bergdall, 'Institutional Learning in a Process-Orientated Programme: Monitoring and Evaluation of the Community Empowerment Programme in South Wallo, Ethiopia'.

27. DGIS, 'Evaluation of SNV Country Programmes in Benin and in Nepal: Perception Study at the Village Level. A Guide on the Methods to be Used'.

28. ETC, 'The Perceptions of the Target Groups on the Kenyan–Dutch Cooperation with Regard to Women and Development in Migori and Homa Bay Districts'.

29. Volker Steigerwald, 'Capacity Development and Impact Assessment: Issues and Concerns for Governmental Technical Cooperation'.

30. Maria Christina Garcia, 'Evaluation of the Impact of an Education and a Malaria Programme'.

31. Jürg Meichle, 'Summary of Problems, Weaknesses and Lessons Learned of a Small NGO Implementing/Improving Simple Monitoring and Evaluation Instruments'.

32. Ramesh Singh, Navaraj Gyanwali, Uddhav Bhattarai and Jane Singh, 'Impact Assessment: ACTIONAID Nepal's Experience'.

33. Hugh Goyder, 'Participatory Impact Assessment – Some Initial Findings from ACTIONAID Ghana'.

34. Salil Shetty, 'Development Project in Assessing Empowerment'.

35. Isa Ferreira, 'Impacts of Systems of Monitoring Adopted in Brazil: The Case of Pojecto Viva a Vida'.

36. Marie Therese Feuerstern, 'Papua New Guinea – Conflict, Multiple Deprivations and Unexpected Outcomes'.

37. Anne Owiti, 'Report of Kebera Community Self-Help Programme'.

38. Phosiso Sola, 'Impact Assessment Research Process in Zimbabwe'.

39. Fundacion Cordes, 'Evaluation of Impact of Accompaniment to the Communities Process'.

40. Anup Kumar Dash, 'Presentation of CYSD's Experiences with Impact Assessment'.

41. Siapha, Kamara and Chris Roche, 'A Participatory Impact Assessment and Advocacy Project for Poverty Alleviation in Northern Ghana'.

42. Tahera Yasmin, 'Partnership and Preparedness'.

43. Yvonne Es, Jan Neggers and Floris Blankenberg, 'Impact Assessment: Making the Most of What You've Got'.

44. Margaret Newens and Chris Roche, 'Evaluating Social Development: Initiatives and Experience in Oxfam'.

Appendix 2

List of Workshop Participants

Binoy Acharya
PRIA
India

Basem Dahab Ali
Centre for Development Studies
Egypt

Lucilla Cuadra Arguello
Juan XXIII
Nicaragua

Catherine Arnold
Centre for Development Studies
Swansea, UK

Paul Beggan
APSO – Agency for Personnel
Services Overseas
Ireland

Maria Lucia Bellacanta
CERIS
Brazil

Max van den Berg
Novib
The Netherlands

Terry Bergdall
Centre For Development Studies
Swansea, UK

Cor van Beuningen
Bilance
The Netherlands

Floris Blankenberg
Novib
The Netherlands

Kees Biekart
Transnational Institute
The Netherlands

Elizabeth Wade-Brown
CAFOD
London, UK

Alex Bush
ITDG – Intermediate Technology
Development Group
Rugby, UK

Andrew Clayton
INTRAC
Oxford, UK

Anne Coles
Department for International
Development
London, UK

Anup Kumar Dash
CYSD
India

Rick Davies
Centre For Development Studies
Swansea, UK

Hans Dehaan
SNV – Netherlands Development
Organisation
The Netherlands

Qasim Deiri
Near East Foundation – Jordan
Jordan

Martin Dütting
Misereor
Germany

Tessa Edlemann
Delta
South Africa

Michael Edwards
London, UK

Yvonne Es
Novib
The Netherlands

Petra Feil
Misereor
Germany

Isa Ferreira
Save the Children Fund
Brazil

Marie Therese Feuerstein
London, UK

Alan Fowler
Philippines

Claudia Fumo
World Bank
USA

Maria Christina Garcia
CINDE
Colombia

Ali Abuel Gasim
Save the Children Fund
Sudan

Dharam Ghai
UNRISD
Switzerland

Foinnuala Gilsenan
Trocaire
Ireland

Hugh Goyder
ACTIONAID
London, UK

Dieneke ve GROOT
ICCO – Interchurch Organisation for
Development Cooperation
The Netherlands

Caroline Harper
Save the Children Fund
London, UK

Mick Howes
Institute of Development Studies
Brighton, UK

Martina Hunt
INTRAC
Oxford, UK

Siapha Kamara
ISODEC Integrated Social
Development Centre
Ghana

Peter van Keijzer
Bilance
The Netherlands

Linda Kelly
CAA – Community Aid Abroad
Australia

Patrick Kilby
Community Aid Abroad
Australia

Anne Kooistra
Novib
The Netherlands

Bernadette Kyany'a
Premise
Kenya

George Kurian
Centre for Youth and Social
Development
India

Bram van Leeuwen
ICCO – Interchurch Organisation for
Development Cooperation
The Netherlands

Ronald Lucardie
Bilance
The Netherlands

Jürg Meichle
Foundation Vivamos Mejor
Switzerland

Anna Minj
CARITAS
Bangladesh

Jan Neggers
Novib
The Netherlands

Margaret Newens
Oxfam
Oxford, UK

Peter Oakley
Centre for Development Studies
Swansea, UK

Frances O'Gorman
Brazil

M. Oomen
DGIS
The Netherlands

Anne Owiti
Kibera Community Self Help
Programmes (KCSHP)
Kenya

Fernando Penaranda
CINDE
Colombia

Ann Maria Philippi
Fundacion De Vida Rural
Chile

Brian Pratt
INTRAC
Oxford, UK

Laura Renshaw
Oxfam
USA

Enrique Reyes
Fundacion CORDES
El Salvador

Chris Roche
Oxfam
Oxford, UK

Jo Rowlands
Voluntary Service Overseas
London, UK

Frances Rubin
Oxford, UK

Paul Ryder
INTRAC
Oxford, UK

Claudia Schwegmann
AEGH
Germany

Md. Shahabuddin
Proshika
Bangladesh

Salil Shetty
ACTIONAID
Kenya

Beng Simeth
Redd Barna
Cambodia

Ramesh Singh
ACTIONAID
Nepal

Phosiso Sola
Environment and Development
Agency (ENDA)
Zimbabwe

Karin Stahl
Brot Fur die Weld
Germany

Volker Steigerwald
GTZ – German Agency for Technical
Cooperation
Germany

Anders Turnold
Norwegian Church Aid
Norway

Rob Visser
DGIS
The Netherlands

Jan Vloet
SNV – Netherlands Development
Organisation
The Netherlands

Hettie Walters
Gender and Development Training
Centre
The Netherlands

Christel Wasiek
AGEH – Association for
Development Cooperation
Germany

Jan Willem van der Raad
Oxfam – Solidariteit
Belgium

Peter Wood
Redd Barna
Norway

Tahera Yasmin
Oxfam
Bangladesh

L. Zuidberg
DGIS
The Netherlands

Bibliography

Barbedette, L. et al. (1995) *Charter for Evaluations Made During Development Work*, Paris: Fondation de France.

Baster, N. (1972) *Measuring Social Development*, Frank Cass.

Beaudoux, E. et al. (1992) *Supporting Development Action*, London: Macmillan.

Bebbington, A. et al. (1994a) *Strengthening the Partnership: Evaluation of the Finnish NGO Programme: Country Case Study, Nicaragua*, Helsinki: ODI/ IDS University of Helsinki.

Bebbington, A. et al. (1994b) *Strengthening the Partnership: Evaluation of the Finnish NGO Programme, Country Case Study: Uganda*, Helsinki: ODI/IDS University of Helsinki.

Beets, N. et al. (1988) '"Big and Still Beautiful" Enquiry into the Efficiency and Effectiveness of Three Big NGOs in South Asia', The Hague: DGIS/ Novib.

Bhasin, K. (1985) *Empowering Women*, Rome: FAO.

Bilance (1991/94) 'Country Programme Impact Studies', Oegstgeest.

Blankenberg, F. (1995a) Oxfam UK/I and Novib Methods of Impact Assessment Research Programme, Resource Pack and Discussion Paper for the Case Studies Phase, The Hague: Novib.

Blankenberg, F. (1995b) 'The Role of Planning, Monitoring and Evaluation', The Hague: Novib.

Booth, D. (ed.) (1995) *Re-thinking Social Development: Theory, Research and Practice*, Harlow: Longmans.

Boyden, J. and Ennew, J. (eds.) (1997) *Children in Focus – a Manual for Participatory Research with Children*, Stockholm: Rädda Barnen.

Brown, D. (1994) 'Strategies of Social Development: Non-Governmental Organisations and the Limitations of the Freirean Approach', Reading: AERDD University of Reading.

Burkey, S. (1993) *People First: A Guide to Self-Reliant Development*, London: Zed Books.

CARE (1994) 'Evaluation of the Economic and Social Benefits of Income Generation Projects', Bangladesh.

Carlsson, J. et.al. (1994) *The Political Economy of Evaluation*, London: Macmillan.

Carmen, R. (1996) *Autonomous Development*, London: Zed Books.

Carroll, T. (1992) *Intermediary NGOs*, Connecticut: Kumarian Press.

Carvalho, S. and White, H. (1995) 'Performance Indicators to Monitor Poverty Reduction', Washington DC: World Bank.

Casley, D. and Kumar, K. (1987) *Project Monitoring and Evaluation in Agriculture*, Washington DC: World Bank/ Johns Hopkins University Press.

Cassen, R. (1994) *Does Aid Work?*, Oxford: Clarenden Press, 2nd edition.

Cebemo/Bilance (1994) 'Sustainable Agriculture: A Way of Life', Oegstgeest.

Cernea, M. (1985) *Putting People First: Sociological Variables in Rural Development*, Oxford: Oxford University Press.

Chambers, R. (1997) *Whose Reality Counts? Putting the first last*, Intermediate Technology: London.

Chambers, R. (1983) *Rural Development: Putting the Last First*, Harlow: Longmans.

Clayton, E. and Petry, F. (1983) 'Monitoring Systems for Agricultural and Rural Development Projects', Rome: FAO.

Cohen, J. and Uphoff, N. (1977) *Rural Development Participation*, New York: Cornell University Press.

Community Development Journal. (1991) *Evaluation of Social Development Projects*, Vol. 26, no. 4, Oxford: Oxford University Press.

Conyers, D. (1982) *Introduction to Social Planning in the Third World*, Chichester: John Wiley.

Cornia, G. et al. (1992) *Africa's Recovery in the 1990s*, London: Macmillan.

Craig, G. and Mayo, M. (1994) *Community Empowerment*, London: Zed Books.

Damodaram, K. (1988) 'The Qualitative Evaluation of Rural Social Development', Reading: AERDD Reading University.

DANIDA (1995) 'Methods for the Evaluation of Poverty Orientated Aid Interventions', Copenhagen: Ministry of Foreign Affairs.

Davies, R. (1995a) 'An Evolutionary Approach to Facilitating Organisational Learning: An Experiment by the Christian Commission for Development in Bangladesh', CDS: Swansea University.

Davies, R. (1995b) 'The Management of Diversity in NGO Development Programmes', CDS: Swansea University.

Davies, R. (1996) 'Donor Information Demands and NGO Institutional Development', CDS: Swansea University.

Dawson, E. (1995a) 'Novib and Oxfam UK/I Impact Assessment Research Programme, Phase III – West Africa', Oxford: Oxfam.

Dawson, E. (1995b) 'Women, Gender and Impact Assessment: A Discussion Paper', Oxford: Oxfam.

Devine, J. (1996) 'NGOs: Changing Fashion or Fashioning Change?', Bath: CDS University of Bath.

Dey, K. and Westendorff, D. (1995) *Their Choice or Yours: Global Forces or Local Voices,* Geneva: UNRISD.

Dey, K. and Westendorff, D. (1996) 'Getting Down to Grass Roots Level: A Community Perspective on Social Development', *Development in Practice,* vol. 6, no. 3.

DFID (1997) 'Project Impact on Livelihood and Farming Systems', New Delhi.

Dutch Government (1995) 'With Quality in Mind: Cebemo, Hivos, ICCO and Novib Impact Study', The Hague: Ministry of Foreign Affairs.

Dütting, M. et al. (1991) 'Evaluations in the Churches' Development Cooperation', Stuttgart: ADKED/MISEREOR.

Edwards, M. (1996) *NGO Performance – What Breeds Success?,* London: SCF.

Edwards, M. and Hulme, D. eds, (1992) *Making a Difference: NGOs and Development in a Changing World,* London: Earthscan/SCF.

Edwards, M. and Hulme, D. eds, (1995) *Non-Governmental Organisations – Performance and Accountability,* London: Earthscan/SCF.

Emmerij, L. (1996) 'Globalisation. Paper presented at IILS Seminar on Social Exclusion', New York, May.

Esteva, A. (1992) 'Development' in Sachs W (ed.) *Development Dictionary,* London: Zed Books.

Feuerstein, M. T. (1986) *Partners in Evaluation,* London: Macmillan.

Flinterman, C. et al. (1992) 'SINAKHO "We can do it!" The Role of Non-Governmental Organisations in the Building of a Just and Democratic South Africa', The Hague: DGIS/Cebemo/ICCO.

Foster-Carter, A. (1974) 'Neo-marxist Approaches to Development and Underdevelopment' in De Kadt, E. and Williams, G. (eds.) *Sociology and Development,* London: Tavistock.

Fowler, A. (1997) *Striking a Balance: A Guide to Making NGO's Effective in International Development*, London: Earthscan/INTRAC.

Franco, F. et al. (1993) 'Empowerment through Entitlemen't, The Hague: Cebemo/DGIS.

Frank, A. (1967) *Capitalism and development in Latin America*, Monthly Review Press.

Freire, P. (1974) *Education: The Practice of Freedom*, Penguin.

Friedmann, J. (1992) *Empowerment: The Politics of Alternative Development*, Oxford: Blackwell.

Freire, P. (1972) *Pedagogy of the Oppressed*, Penguin.

Galjart, B. (1981) 'Counterdevelopment', *Community Development Journal*, vol. 16 , no. 2.

Galjart, B. and Buijs, D. (eds.) (1982) *Participation of the Poor in Development*, Leiden: Institute of Cultural and Social Studies, University of Leiden.

Gardner, K. and Lewis, D. (1996) *Anthropology, Development and the Post-Modern Challenge*, London: Pluto Press.

Gardner, R.K. and Judd, H.O. (1963) *The Development of Social Administration*, Oxford: Oxford University Press.

Gaspar, K. et al. (1994) 'Peoples' Empowerment Through Cooperatives', The Hague: DGIS/ Cebemo.

Ghai, D. (1977) Participatory Organisations of the Rural Poor, Geneva: ILO.

Gore, C. and Figueiredo, J. B. (eds.) (1996) *Social Exclusion and Anti-Poverty Strategies*, Geneva: International Institute for Labour Studies.

Gosling, L. and Edwards, M. (1995) *Toolkits: A Practical Guide to Assessment Monitoring, Review and Evaluation*, London: SCF.

Goyder, H. (1995) 'New Approaches to Participatory Impact Assessment', London: ACTIONAID.

Guba, E. and Lincoln, Y. (1989) *Fourth Generation Evaluation*, California: SAGE.

Hardeman, J. et al. (1993) 'Se Dice...Exigimos Creditos Agiles y Oportunos', The Hague: GIS/ ICCO.

Hardiman, M. and Midgley, J. (1982) *The Social Dimensions of Development: Social Policy and Planning in the Third World*, Chichester: John Wiley

Heidenreich, A. (1995) 'NGO Country Profile: Uganda', Oegestgeest: GOM.

Hivos (1993) 'Towards a Hivos Style of Intervention', The Hague.

Hopkins, R. (1994) Impact Assessment: Overview and methods, Oxfam/Novib.

Hopkins, R. (1995a) 'The Experience of Latin American NGOs', The Hague: Oxfam/Novib.

Hopkins, R. (1995b) 'Impact Assessment: Overview and Methods of Application', Oxford: Oxfam/ Novib.

Howes, M. (1991) 'Linking Paradigms and Practise: Key Issues in the Appraisal, Monitoring and Evaluation of British NGO Projects', Sussex: IDS.

Jones, H. (1990) *Social Welfare in the Third World*, London: Macmillan.

Jones, J. (1981) *Social Development: Conceptual, Methodological and Policy Issues*, New York: St. Martin's Press.

Kaplan, A. (1996) *The Development Practitioner's Handbook*, London: Pluto Press.

Khan, S. (1994) 'Ranking Social Development Indicators', London: ACTION-AID.

Kliest, T. et al. (1995) 'Evaluation and Monitoring', The Hague: DGIS.

Korten, D. and Alfonso, F. (1981) *Bureaucracy and the Poor*, Manila: Asian Institute of Management.

Kreuse (1996) Centre for Partnership and Development, Oslo: personal communication.

Kutenbrouwer, J. (1977) 'Continuity and Discontinuity in Community Development Theory', The Hague: Institute of Social Studies.

Lefevre, P. and Garcia, C. (1997) 'Experiences, Perceptions and Expectations of Local Project Actors in Monitoring and Evaluation', *Journal of International Development*, vol. 9, no. 1, pp. 1-20.

Lichfield, N. (1996) *Community Impact Evaluation*, London: UCL Press.

Loflan, J. (1971) *Analysing Social Settings*, Belmont: California Wadsworth Press.

Long, N. (1976) *Introduction to the Sociology of Rural Development*, London: Tavistock.

Macpherson, S. (1982) *Social Policy in the Third World*, Wheatsheaf Books.

Macpherson, S. and Midgley, J. (1987) *Comparative Social Policy and the Third World*, Wheatsheaf Books.

Mansfield, D. (1996) 'Review of SCF Evaluation Reports', London: SCF.

Marsden, D. (1990) 'The Meaning of Social Development', Swansea: Centre for Development Studies.

Marsden, D. and Oakley, P. (1990) *Evaluating Social Development Projects*, Oxford: Oxfam.

Marsden, D., Oakley, P. and Pratt, B. (1994) *Measuring the Process: Guidelines for Evaluating Social Development*, Oxford: INTRAC.

Mbogori, E. and Taylor, B. (1995) 'Impact Evaluation: A New Path for Developing an Equitable, Participatory, Sustainable Approach to Evaluating for Impact', Lesotho: MWENGO/ Partnership Africa Canada.

McGranaham, D. et al. (1990) Qualitative Indicators of Development, Geneva: UNRISD.

Midgley, J. (1995) *Social Development: The Developmental Perspective in Social Welfare*, California: SAGE.

Mkandawire, T. (1994) 'Adjustment, Political Conditionality and Democratisation in Africa' in Cornia G. (ed.) *From Adjustment to Development in Africa*, London: Macmillan.

Montgomery, R. (1995) 'Stakeholder Analysis', Swansea: Centre for Development Studies.

Moris, J. and Copestake, J. (1993) 'Qualitative Enquiry for Rural Development', London: ODI.

Moser, C. (1991) *Gender Planning and Development*, London: Routledge.

Neggers, J. and Wils, F. (1987) 'Self-Evaluation among Local Organisations and NGDOs in Third World Countries, Problems and Prospects', The Hague: Novib/ ISS.

Nielson, H. (n.d.) 'Monitoring the Development Intervention: An Alternative Approach to Impact Evaluation', Denmark: Aalborg University.

Oakley, P. (1988a) 'Conceptual Problems of the Monitoring and Evaluation of Qualitative Objectives', *Community Development Journal*, vol. 23, no. 1, pp 3–11.

Oakley, P. (1988b) 'The Monitoring and Evaluation of Participation', Rome: FAO.

Oakley, P. and Winder, D. (1981) 'The Concept and Practise of Rural Social Development: Current Trends in Latin America and India', *Manchester Papers on Development*, no. 1.

Ocampo-Cobos, A. (1993) 'The Empowering Dimension of Social Evaluation: Concepts, Controversies and Challenges', Swansea: Centre for Development Studies.

ODA (1993) *Social Development Handbook*, London.

ODA (1995) 'Project Monitoring and Impact Systems in India', London.

ODA (1995–96) 'Record of the Working Group Discussion on Monitoring and Impact Review Systems', London.

ODI (1996) 'The Impact of NGO Development Projects', *Briefing Paper,* London.

OECD (1993) *Non-governmental organisations and governments: Stakeholders for development,* Paris: OECD Development Centre.

OECD (1994) 'Promoting Participatory Development: From Advocacy to Action', Paris.

Ondam, B. et al. (1988) 'Joint Evaluation of the Cebemo Programme in Thailand', The Hague: DGIS/Cebemo.

Ostberg, S. (1994) 'A Checklist for Measuring the Performance of Development Projects, A Method Adopted by BIFO to Promote an Evaluation System', Stockholm: BIFO.

Parlett, M. and Hamilton, D. (1972) 'Evaluation as Illumination', University of Edinburgh.

Partnership Africa Canada (1995) 'Impact Evaluation', Internal Report, Ottawa.

Patton, (1987) *How to Use Qualitative Methods in Evaluation,* California: SAGE.

PLAN International. (1995) 'Corporate Planning, Monitoring and Evaluation', Woking.

Popple, K. and Shaw, M. (1997) 'Community Development and Social Movements', *Community Development Journal,* vol. 32, no. 3.

Pratt, B. and Boyden, J. (1985) *The Field Directors' Handbook,* Oxford: Oxfam.

Pretty, J. (1994) 'Alternative Systems of Inquiry for a Sustainable Agriculture', *IDS Bulletin,* vol. 25, no. 2.

Priester, M. et al. (1995) 'With Quality in Mind: Final Report on the Measures Taken by Cebemo, Hivos, ICCO and Novib in Response to the Impact Study', Amsterdam: GOM.

Putnam, D. with Leonardi, R. and Nanetti, R. (1993) *Making Democracy Work: Civic Traditions in Modern Italy*, Princeton: Princeton University Press.

Rahman, A. (1989) 'Glimpses of Another Africa', ILO.

Rahman, A. (1993) *People's Development*, London: Zed Books.

Richards, H. (1985) *The Evaluation of Cultural Action*, London: Macmillan.

Richards, P. (1985) *Indigenous Agricultural Revolution*, London: Hutchinson.

Riddell, R. (1990) 'Judging Success: Evaluating NGO Approaches to Alleviating Poverty in Developing Countries', London: ODI

Riddell, R. et al. (1994) 'Strengthening the Partnership: Evaluation of the Finnish NGO Programme', Helsinki: ODI/IDS Uiversity of Helsinki.

Rifkin, S. and Bichmann, W. (1988) 'On Measuring Participation', *Social Science and Medicine*, vol. 6, no. 9, pp. 931–40.

Robinson, M. and Thin, N. (1993) 'Project Evaluation: A Guide for NGOs', Glasgow: ODA.

Roche, C. (1994) 'Operationality in Turbulence', *Development in Practice*, vol. 4, no. 3.

Rowlands, J. (1997) 'Questioning Empowerment', Oxford: Oxfam.

Ruxton, R. (1995) 'Participation in Impact Assessment', Oxford: Oxfam.

Sahn, D. et al. (1995) 'Methods for Evaluation of Poverty Oriented Aid Interventions', Copenhagen: DANIDA.

Salmon, L. (1989) 'Beneficiary Assessment', Washington DC: World Bank.

Shetty, S. (1994) 'Development Project in Assessing Empowerment'. New Delhi: Society for Participatory Research Institute for Asia.

Singer, H. and Jolly, R. (1995) 'Fifty Years On: The UN and Economic and Social Development', Sussex: IDS.

Smillie, I. (1995) *The Alms Bazaar: Altruism under fire – Non-Profit Organisations and International Development*, London: IT Publications.

Squire, R. (1994) 'Evaluating the Effectiveness of Poverty Alleviation Programmes', Washington DC: World Bank.

Stiefel, M. and Wolfe, M. (1994) *A Voice for the Excluded*, London: Zed Books.

Surr, M.A. (1995) 'Evaluation of NGOs in Development Programmes: Synthesis Report', London: ODA.

Tendler, J. (1982) 'Turning Private Voluntary Organisations into Development Agencies', USAID Programme Evaluation, Washington DC: USAID.

Tilakaratna, S. (1989) 'The Animator in Participatory Rural Development', Geneva: ILO.

Umutesi, B. (1995) 'Final Workshop to Phase 1 of the PME Dialogue Process: Declaration of Key Findings', Bleyerheide.

UN (1989) 'Guiding Principles for Developmental Social Welfare Policies', New York.

UN (1995) 'World Summit for Social Development', New York.

UNRISD (1994) 'The Crisis of Social Development in the 1990s: Preparing for the World Social Summit', Geneva.

UNRISD (1995a) 'Adjustment, Globalisation and Social Development', Geneva.

UNRISD (1995b) 'Monitoring Social Progress in the 1990s', Geneva.

Uphoff, N. (1989) 'A Field Methodology for Participatory Self-Evaluation of People's Participation Groups', Rome: FAO.

Valadez, J. and Bamberger, M. (1994) 'Monitoring and Evaluating Social Programs in Developing Countries', Washington: EDI Development Studies.

van Cranenburgh, O. and Sasse, R. (1995) 'NGO Country Profile: Tanzania', Oegestgeest: GOM.

van Eyken, W. (1991) 'The Concept and Process of Empowerment', The Hague: Bernard van Leer Foundation.

van Roosmalen, H. and Guimaraes, J. (1995) 'NGO Country Profile: Bangladesh', Oegestgeest: GOM.

Wallace, T. et al. (1996) 'Influences on NGO Programme and Project Management', Birmingham, Development Administration Group, University of Birmingham.

Walters, H., Hermans, A. and Van der Hel, M. (1995) 'Monitoring and Evaluation from a Gender Perspective', The Hague: SNV.

Wardle, C. (1996) 'Wider Impact Study, Tanzania: Draft design and Plan', Concern.

Wehkamp, A. and Blankenberg, F. (1995) 'Report of the Workshop to Introduce the Research Programme on Methods of Impact Assessment at CYSD, India', Bhubaneswar/Puri, The Hague: Novib.

Wehkamp, A. and Blankenberg, F. (1995) Report of the Workshop to Introduce the Research Programme on Methods of Impact Assessment at ENDA, Zimbabwe, Harare/The Hague: Novib.

Westendorff, D. and Ghai, D. (1993) 'Monitoring Social Progress in the 1990s', Geneva: UNRISD.

Wils, F. et al. (1993) 'Big NGDOs in Latin America', The Hague: DGIS/ Novib.

Wolfe, M. (1996) *Elusive Development*, London: Zed Books.

World Bank (1975) *World Development Report*, Washington DC.

World Bank (1994) 'The World Bank and Participation', Washington DC.

World Bank (1994) 'Advancing Social Development', Washington DC.

World Bank (1996) *Participation Sourcebook*, Washington DC.

World Bank (1997) *World Development Report,* Washington DC.

World Vision (n.d.) 'Monitoring and Evaluation Manual', World Vision.

Zadek, S. and Evans, R. (1993) *Social Audit*, London: New Economics Foundation.